Follow Him in All Things

Asking and Answering Life's Ultimate Questions

Follow Him in All Things

Asking and Answering Life's Ultimate Questions

By:

Hollis McGehee

Grace Publishing
Ocean Springs, Mississippi

Contents

Part One

Part two

Part three

Preface

I WAS BORN INTO THIS WORLD on December 3, 1953. In April 1966, I was born a second time, born from above into God's kingdom. Five decades later I am beginning to understand my purpose and place in life. I am not here by accident. God put me here for a purpose. My purpose is to love and honor God with all that I am and all that I have.

God's purpose is the same for all of us. None of us is here by accident. We were each born into our particular place and time for the chief purpose of loving and honoring God. Missing the very purpose of our lives is the greatest of all tragedies.

A. W. Tozer's *The Pursuit of God* played a prominent role in my awakening to God's very clear purpose for life. The purpose here in this writing is plain, simple, but life altering: pointing each of us to live with Jesus Christ as the centerpiece of everything! May we each know our purpose and live our lives according to our purpose.

Calling one and all to lives centered in Christ is the heart of this book. Jesus said if anyone would come after Him, they must deny themselves, take up their cross daily, and follow Him (see Luke 9:23). Following after Jesus requires us to take a narrow path that is filled with challenges; by trusting fully in Him, it is one characterized by great joy and deep peace.

Following after Jesus is not a road for a few "especially spiritual Christians"; it is the journey for all who are in Christ. Christ first is the only path for all; there is no back-up plan. A life committed to honoring God by following Christ is our very reason for living; what a tragedy it would be to miss the very purpose of our lives.

Through this book, I hope to challenge each of us, by God's grace, to live a Christ-centered life as we die to self daily. It is my goal and desire to give this book to as many as God enables so we all are encouraged to live with Jesus Christ as the center point and foundation for all of life, time, and eternity. May our hearts and all that we have and all that we are be abandoned to Him!

Introduction

²³ "If anyone would come after me, let him deny himself and take up his cross daily and follow me. ²⁴ For whoever would save his life will lose it, but whoever loses his life for my sake will save it. ²⁵ For what does it profit a man if he gains the whole world and loses or forfeits himself?"

(Luke 9:23-25)

FOLLOWING AFTER CHRIST IS SETTING aside self and embracing a life of love and service to God and those He brings across our path: that is to say, a life centered in Christ. Christ-centered and self-centered are distinctly different life paths of which one can say, "Never the twain shall meet."[1]

Contrary to what many claim, committing to following Christ does not assure you of happiness, success, wealth, a perfect family, or job security. In fact, Jesus warned that following Him is neither easy nor popular. Jesus did promise us that in giving (losing, laying down) our life for Him, we will find real life. Anyone who is truly following after Christ can give a strong amen to real life in Christ Jesus.

Modern Christianity considers Christ-centered living as some form of radicalism. In reality, the life I speak of here is simply basic Christianity as defined by Jesus. If you desire to really pursue a deeper relationship with Jesus (what possible excuse might we offer for not?), then I pray you will find encouragement here.

God did not send Jesus to die on a cross just to save us from hell. Jesus came to reconcile us to God the Father that we might honor God with and in our lives, to live fully for God, who is the source of all creation.

> [36] For from him and through him and to him
> are all things. To him be glory forever. Amen.
> *(Romans 11:36)*

Part One

Who Do You Say God Is?

Chapter 1

Knowing and Trusting God

I AWOKE WITH THESE WORDS OF praise flowing from my heart out through my lips: "You're a good, good Father / It's who you are / You are perfect in all of your ways."[2] Knowing God is perfect in all of His ways is the most important thing knowable! It is vitally important for us to think right things about God and come to know Him for who He really is, perfect in all of His ways. Knowing God for who He really is will transform our lives and lead us to fully trust Him; knowing and trusting God is key to loving and following Him.

The more we know and trust God, the better we worship and serve God with growing intimacy and focus. Our worship of God is key to encountering the Person of God. Encountering, loving, and worshipping the Person of God (Father, Son, and Holy Spirit) is our reason for existence. God does not need, us but we desperately need Him! Being in a loving, worshipful relationship with Him and loving His people are the reasons for our existence—it is for those very purposes He created us.

When we begin to think right thoughts about who God is, we will, by His grace, begin to live right lives in the light of God's holiness and perfection. Having a proper view of God opens the doorway to a proper view of ourselves. When we see God for who He is and see ourselves in the light of Him, one of two things happen: (a) we become disheartened and turn back to being a little religious, satisfied with living a lukewarm existence, going back to the way "we have always done things"; or (b) we begin to seriously seek after the "crucified life,"[3] where Christ is everything, where we truly know we are His, we belong to Him, and nothing else matters. We live abandoned to Jesus Christ.

The very moment we die to self is the moment we truly begin to live—living the abundant life Christ died to give us! This is not something that happens one day and we are "through." The Apostle Paul, after knowing and serving Jesus Christ for many years through many devastating challenges, said,

> [10] And this, so that I may know Him [experientially, becoming more thoroughly acquainted with Him, understanding the remarkable wonders of His Person more completely] and [in that same way experience] the power of His resurrection [which overflows and is active in believers], and [that I may share] the fellowship of His sufferings, by being continually transformed [inwardly into His likeness even] to His death [dying as He did].
>
> *(Philippians 3:10, AMP)*

In my seventh decade of life, I have finally begun to see God for who He is. The more I see of God, the more I want to know Him! The journey to a deeper knowledge of God is just beginning for me; the more I know Him, the more I love Him; and the more I love Him, the more I want to know Him. He is beginning to become in my thoughts what He has always been: everything!

Coming to know God for who He really is radically changes the dynamics of our daily lives. When we know that the very God who created everything is personally with each one of us, loves us, and has promised never to leave us—nothing could possibly be sweeter, nothing could be more important. There is no greater thing than knowing God!

> [31] What then shall we say to these things? If God is for us, who can be against us? [32] He who did not spare his own Son but gave him up for us all, how will he not also with him graciously give us all things?
>
> *(Romans 8:31-32)*

Life is a great joy today because I know who God is and who I am in Christ. I have discovered my purpose in life, and I have set my sights on the one true destination of a life that counts, Christ Himself—more of Him, less of me!

Why has it taken me so long to learn the ultimate importance of knowing Jesus? I do not know the answer to the question, but because God is perfect in all of His ways, I do not lament that I am learning these truths late. However, I do encourage you to grasp the fullness of God as early as possible. There were many years I wandered with little or no purpose. Rather than getting bogged down in the why of God's timing

(I think the enemy would love for me to cry over those lost years), my focus is rejoicing in what God is teaching me now as I seek a deeper walk with Christ. After all, God is in control, and His timing, like everything else about Him, is perfect in every way. God is revealing Himself to me at the perfect time according to His great plan. It is my fervent prayer that He will use this book to help you and me in our pursuit of God.

Knowing God leads to trusting God. Trusting God in all circumstances is one of God's most important and beautiful gifts. When we know God loves us and His purpose in all things is for our good, we begin to fully experience true peace, joy, and contentment. We cease to agonize over why things happen the way they do; we look to God instead of our circumstances. Knowing God, not man, is ultimately in charge helps us to develop an unoffendable heart. Someone else may have intended harm for us, but God will work it for our good so we refuse to get angry and can even give thanks in all circumstances. God is growing us up in Him.

> [2] Count it all joy, my brothers, when you meet trials of various kinds, [3] for you know that the testing of your faith produces steadfastness. [4] And let steadfastness have its full effect, that you may be perfect and complete, lacking in nothing.
>
> *(James 1:2-4)*

Each of us experiences challenges every day. God uses life's challenges to shape and mold us into the people He created us to be. Knowing, trusting, and following God day by day leads to a transformation[4] from the "old you" to revealing Christ in you. The most radical procedure in our makeover involves self/

pride. Self (selfish, self-centered, me, my, mine) is the greatest sin that must be removed from and conquered within each of us; it is a form of spiritual pride (the opposite of being "poor in spirit," Matthew 5:3). Spiritual pride is any sense that we are good enough to save ourselves or even to contribute the least bit to our place in God through Christ. Pride is every thought and attitude that adopts or incorporates any such "self" thought; pride is not from God.

God has to trim away all thoughts of pride, self-sufficiency, and self-adequacy from us to show us our complete dependence upon Him. This cutting away of pride is a lifelong process. It is a form of pruning; it is never easy or pleasant at the moment, but it is always productive if we trust God in the process. My experience has been that it happens like this: "Lord, this hurts and I don't know what You are doing, but I do know You love me and You want what is best for me. Lord, I trust You." This is the same deep trust Jesus expressed to the Father when He said,

> [42] Father, if you are willing, remove this cup from me. Nevertheless, not my will, but yours, be done.
>
> *(Luke 22:42)*

Jesus Christ is our example in all things.

The storms that blow into our lives are used by God to reveal the deeper truth of who God is and who we are. How we respond to the storms or tests in life has a great impact on the course of our lives.

> [35] On that day, when evening had come, [Jesus] said to them, "Let us go across to the other side." [36] And leaving the crowd, they took him with them in the boat, just as he was. And

other boats were with him. [37] And a great wind-storm arose, and the waves were breaking into the boat, so that the boat was already filling. [38] But he was in the stern, asleep on the cushion. And they woke him and said to him, "Teacher, do you not care that we are perishing?" [39] And he awoke and rebuked the wind and said to the sea, "Peace! Be still!" And the wind ceased, and there was a great calm. [40] He said to them, "Why are you so afraid? Have you still no faith?" [41] And they were filled with great fear and said to one another, "Who then is this, that even the wind and the sea obey him?"

(Mark 4:35-41)

The disciples went from a time of great doubting to a deeper knowledge of God. They went from fear and trembling in the face of the storm to reverential fear and honor for the Master of the sea. Charles Swindoll has said, "I am convinced that life is 10 percent what happens to me and 90 percent of how I react to it." How we respond is determined by our view of God, and we have to get the right view of God—that is my heart's burning desire for you and for me.

I have to acknowledge here that much of my life has consisted of a very self-centered, selfish, and self-destructive path that has wounded myself and many others. The pain of my failures is still deeply felt by me and those impacted. I must and do accept full responsibility for my failures and the resulting harm. However, it is not the failures that I wish to emphasize but rather the work of God's grace in my life.

My report is "God loves you, He has a plan for your life, His plan is through the finished work of the Savior Jesus Christ. He has called us into a deep love relationship with Him. The right relationship with God is one where we progressively grow in our knowledge of and our love for Him. Knowing God leads to trusting God. Trusting God allows life's challenges to shape us into who He wants us to be. With God, the closer we get, the better He looks. We are all sinners, and we all fail. No one will ever be right with God by his or her efforts or actions. Jesus died in our place that we might live through Him, living fully surrendered to God where our daily goal is to die to ourselves and take up our cross and follow Jesus."[5]

I pray that sharing some of my own failures will hopefully help you avoid some of my poor choices and accept your own failures as a means for God to shape you into the person He intends you to be. May we each move forward to living the full Christ-centered life God has set before us.

We can see many examples in Scripture where God used a person's failures to actually help them grow and mature spiritually. I have found that God uses our failures to teach us the ultimate lesson of trusting Him. The clearest statement we have on trusting God is this powerful command and promise:

> [5] *Trust in the LORD with all your heart,*
> *and do not lean on your own understanding.*
>
> [6] *In all your ways acknowledge him,*
> *and he will make straight your paths.*
> (Proverbs 3:5-6)

Trusting in the Lord with all our heart means we learn to do things His way, which is always, without exception, the right and better way. Knowing and trusting God will radically change how we respond to every mountain and molehill we encounter in life.

God uses the events of life to mold us into the people He put us here to be. However, this only happens as we start to know and understand God for who He really is.

Fully trusting God is a major challenge; the largest part of the trusting God challenge is "me." The reason is clear: I am holding out hope that there is some good in me and that I will be able to help God make me better, to help with my salvation. This thought must fully die. "Self" anything (self-righteous, self-centered, self-absorbed, selfish) must die. I have to know that life is one thing: Jesus! It is not and cannot ever be "Jesus plus I did . . ." Today, I know "I dare not trust the sweetest frame but wholly lean on Jesus' name."

We might imagine the picture of Christ's finished work in this way: We are standing in line to pay for our purchases. Jesus takes our place and pays our bill in full. Jesus is disgraced when we, knowing He has paid the bill in full, continue to stand in line and try to pay a bill He has already paid. He wants us to accept Him and His finished work, and we do that by knowing, trusting, and resting in Him—taking our eyes off ourselves and looking unto Him fully and finally!

My Hope Is Built on Nothing Less[6]

My hope is built on nothing less
than Jesus' blood and righteousness.
I dare not truth the sweetest frame,
but wholly lean on Jesus' name.

REFRAIN

On Christ the solid rock I stand,
all other ground is sinking sand;
all other ground is sinking sand.

When Darkness veils His lovely face,
I rest on His unchanging grace.
In every high and stormy gale,
my anchor holds within the veil.

REFRAIN

His oath, His covenant, His blood
support me in the whelming flood.
When all around my soul gives way,
He then is all my hope and stay

REFRAIN

When He shall come with trumpet sound,
O may I then in Him be found!
Dressed in His righteousness alone,
faultless to stand before the throne!

REFRAIN

Prayer to know and trust God more each day:

Heavenly Father, Almighty God, help us to know You are a "good, good Father" and You are perfect in all of your ways. Help us to know we can and must trust You completely, leaning fully on You and trusting in You with all of our hearts. Lord, help us to know we can do nothing without You; we can't even draw a breath except that You have given it to us. Help each of us to build our lives on the reality of who You are. Lord, we want to know you as fully as we can; help us to lay aside any thoughts we have except the truth of who You reveal Yourself to be in Your Word, knowing that whatever happens in our lives, we can and absolutely must rest and trust wholly in You. We pray this in Jesus' holy and precious name.

Amen.

Chapter 2

God Reveals Himself

Living fully for God, being abandoned to God, can start to happen as we begin to see God as He really is. We will never, on this earth, know all of God; if we could know all of God, He would not be God. Yet God reveals to us all we need to know in order to trust, love, worship, and serve Him here. We are not there yet, but we need to seek Him more and more every day. We also have to acknowledge that knowing God is both a daily and a lifelong process. Either we are seeking more of God or we are falling away from Him. Paul, who wrote the majority of the New Testament, acknowledged he was not there yet:

> [10] And this, so that I may know Him [experientially, becoming more thoroughly acquainted with Him, understanding the remarkable wonders of His Person more completely] and [in that same way experience] the power of His resurrection [which overflows and is active in believers], and [that I may share] the

fellowship of His sufferings, by being contin-
ually transformed [inwardly into His likeness
even] to His death [dying as He did].
                                    (Philippians 3:10, AMP)

And so we must know, like Paul, we have not arrived
at full knowledge of God. May we seek to know God
with the same zeal Paul had. God Himself alive and
present in Paul's words fires me up to seek after Him!

Our relationship with God is personal; He reveals
Himself to each of us individually. We certainly can
learn from others who are ahead of us, but to really
encounter and come to know God deeper, we must
have a personal encounter with God Himself. God
wants a personal encounter with you and me. He will
reveal Himself to us more and more as we seek Him in
Scripture, in prayer, and in worship. Corporate worship and Christ-centered sermons and teachings are
tools God uses to draw us closer, but our personal encounter with God is the key to growing in our knowledge of God. Once we catch the beauty and reality of
this personal experience and knowledge of Him, nothing else can compare with Him; nothing else will satisfy. God's presence with each of us exceeds anything
else we will ever experience in this life.

The Holy Bible is God's primary means of revealing Himself to us. We sometimes struggle getting into
this book. The problem is that we do not have right
thoughts about what the Bible is. The Bible should not
be thought of as a book in the normal sense we think
of that word. The Bible is alive, and it is God revealing
Himself to us. Reading the Bible under the direction
of the Holy Spirit is an immediate and real encounter with the Creator of this world. In His Word, God
personally and intimately reveals Himself to us, and
we begin to personally experience and enjoy His real,

joyful, loving, and wise presence in our lives. Scripture is God speaking to us personally at this very moment. God's revelation of Himself is progressive; the more we go to Him, the more He reveals. The more He reveals, the more we love Him. The more we love Him, the more we want to know Him.

The Bible is also a call from God to each of us. He says, "Come to Me through Christ Jesus and live the rest of your life in a personal love relationship with Me." The Bible reveals that God Himself is the initiator of the love and the relationship. We don't have to seek Him; He has been seeking us all along. When we begin to understand the fullness of God's love and call on each of us, life rockets to a whole new level experienced nowhere else nor in anyone else other than the person of God—Father, Son, and Holy Spirit. Knowing God is a lifelong process, but we start that "journey of a thousand miles" with our first step of seeking to know God as He really is in Scripture, prayer, a personal love relationship, and corporate worship as well as other ways.

God is "our Father," and like an earthly father, He wants His children to know Him and love Him. In other words, He is waiting with great love and anticipation for us to respond to His invitation to know and love Him more and more. Like a child seeking to take his first steps, may we move toward Him now by opening His Holy Bible and simply asking God to show Himself to us; He is waiting, and nothing would be more pleasing than for His children to say, "Abba Father, I want to know You better; show Yourself to me."

Jesus asked Peter a simple but penetrating question; it is a question we all must answer: "But who do you say that I am?"

[16]Simon Peter replied, "You are the Christ, the Son of the living God." [17] And Jesus answered him, "Blessed are you, Simon Bar-Jonah! For flesh and blood has not revealed this to you, but my Father who is in heaven.

(Matthew 16:16-17)

God revealed Himself to Peter and He will reveal Himself to us as we seek Him. We have to make knowing God the priority in our lives, wanting God in the same way we want our next breath. David lived in a place where water was precious, and every living creature longs for water. David expressed his longing for God like this:

[1] *As the deer longs for streams of water,*
so I long for you, O God.

[2] *I thirst for God, the living God.*
When can I go and stand before him?
(Psalm 42:1-2, NLT)

We looked at Paul earlier when he was seeking God just as David is here. Paul in effect said to God, "Nothing else matters, Lord. I just want to know You." He said, "I want to know Christ, and by knowing Him to know that there is no righteousness in me." Paul was growing in his knowledge of God, and a significant revelation to him was that nothing we have—no title, no possession, no accolade—amounts to anything before God. Paul showed us how God progressively reveals Himself to us.

[10] that I may know him and the power of his resurrection, and may share his sufferings, becoming like him in his death,[11] that by any

means possible I may attain the resurrection
from the dead.

(Philippians 3:10-11)

Paul said in essence, "I want to know Jesus and become like Him in every way, even in suffering." Paul
went on to show us that growing in our knowledge of
God should never end. We should seek to know Him
more and more every day.

> [12] Not that I have already obtained this or
> am already perfect, but I press on to make it
> my own, because Christ Jesus has made me
> his own. [13] Brothers, I do not consider that
> I have made it my own. But one thing I do:
> forgetting what lies behind and straining for-
> ward to what lies ahead, [14] I press on toward
> the goal for the prize of the upward call of
> God in Christ Jesus.
>
> *(Philippians 3:12-14)*

This is the picture or model we must follow: press-
ing on to know God more and more. God has called
us to Him, and we need to be consumed with the call
of God upon our lives.

God is the consuming passion in my life today. I
want to know Him! I am not there yet, but I am, by
God's amazing grace, on the road to knowing Him
better. This is my prayer for each of us, that we be in-
fected with the burning desire to know Jesus, to want
and long for Him as we desperately seek after a drop
of water in a time of great thirst. As the deer pants for
the water, so our souls long after You, O God!

Prayer to know God more and more as He reveals Himself:

God, help us each to know You love us and want a deeper love relationship with us. You want us to know You as much as we can as we are led deeper and deeper into relationship with You by our Guide, the Holy Spirit. Lord, give us a growing desire to know You more intimately and more fully and to seek this relationship with You in Your Word, in prayer, and in our experience of You personally and with other Christians. Lord, help us to know You. We pray this in the matchless name of Jesus.

Amen.

Chapter 3

Knowing God Reveals Our Purpose in Life

A GOOD FRIEND I HOLD IN high regard recently told me his current job was one of the boxes he wanted to check off in his life. He went on to tell me about the other boxes he hoped to yet check off. I thought to myself, "This guy has lived his whole life with a plan and a purpose." I think it was that day (not very long ago) that I said to myself, "You love the Lord and you want to be of use to Him, but you are not being intentional in living every day on purpose." I made up my mind right then to become more purposeful and more focused on how God would have me to live, what His purposes are for my life, where and how He wants me to serve and glorify Him![7]

As we seek to know God through His Word, prayer, and worship, He honors our efforts by revealing Himself to us. He also shows us a true picture of who we are. Seeing the holiness of God reveals my complete poverty and my desperate need for God. God does not need me, but I (and each of us) desperately need God. This lesson is one demonstrated very powerfully when Jesus confronted religious people in His day who thought they had it all together.

> 15 And as he reclined at table in his house, many tax collectors and sinners were reclining with Jesus and his disciples, for there were many who followed him. 16 And the scribes of the Pharisees, when they saw that he was eating with sinners and tax collectors, said to his disciples, "Why does he eat with tax collectors and sinners?" 17 And when Jesus heard it, he said to them, "Those who are well have no need of a physician, but those who are sick. I came not to call the righteous, but sinners."
>
> *(Mark 2:15-17)*

This story shows us we are all in one of two groups: those who know they need a doctor or those who foolishly think they do not. Lord, thank You for showing us who we really are and our deep need for You.

The more we know God and know ourselves, the clearer we see our life purpose. Knowing God shows us we are each here for a reason; every life has a definite purpose and meaning. I confess I missed this for much of my life; I simply did what was in front of me. Living life without a growing awareness of our purpose leads to a great waste of time and resources. God put each one of us right where we are at this exact time for very specific purposes.

Our ultimate purpose is to love and honor God. He put us here to be in a personal, dynamic love relationship with Him! He wants us to center our lives in Him, loving and serving Him in every way, in all we are and with all we have. This will strike some as extreme selfishness by God; if you know Him, you know this is a great blessing. There is no greater joy than knowing and loving God. Now we see why—it is the very reason for our existence. When a person finds their purpose, they experience completion and it is the source of deep and abiding joy and peace.

One of my heroes, A. W. Tozer, a man of no formal education who lived and died a simple but very driven and intensely focused man, said our purpose is "that we might worship God and enjoy him forever."[8]Here are a few excerpts from the Word of God regarding the purpose of life for every one of us:

> [13] The end of the matter; all has been heard. Fear God and keep his commandments, for this is the whole duty of man.
>
> *(Ecclesiastes 12:13)*

> [31] So, whether you eat or drink, or whatever you do, do all to the glory of God.
>
> *(1 Corinthians 10:31)*

> [1] I appeal to you therefore, brothers, by the mercies of God, to present your bodies as a living sacrifice, holy and acceptable to God, which is your spiritual worship. [2] Do not be conformed to this world, but be transformed by the renewal of your mind, that by testing you may discern what is the will of God, what is good and acceptable and perfect.
>
> *(Romans 12:1-2)*

God says it is our duty to fear God (honor and worship Him as God), to lovingly obey His commandments (love God and our neighbors as ourselves), to do every single thing we do for the glory of God, and to offer our very lives in full surrender to God. *God is our purpose!* We are here to honor and obey God.

Brother Lawrence (Nicolas Herman, a Catholic monk who lived in the 1600s in Paris) was a dishwasher for many years in a Paris monastery. Brother Lawrence said he washed his dishes for the glory of God. He said, "I would not even take up a piece of straw from the ground if I thought he didn't want me to but would run to pick it up out of love for him if that is what he wanted."[9] When you read Brother Lawrence's life story and the joy he experienced daily in God's presence, you know this simple man got what so many have sought for so long in so many wrong ways. I am one of those who was, in the words of a song, "looking for love in all the wrong places" but found love and joy and peace in a growing love relationship with my Creator.

The Westminster Larger Catechism says, "Man's chief and highest end is to glorify God, and fully to enjoy him forever."[10]

It is said that when A. W. Tozer discovered a certain book, his life changed direction and the rest of his life was very focused and purposeful. I think it is safe to say that he did that to me when I found him. A friend handed me A. W. Tozer's *The Pursuit of God*, and my life has never been the same. This book helped me to refocus on what I am here for. Tozer helped me to focus on loving and worshipping God. I am seeking to live the "Worship-Driven Life." The focus and changes in my life are flowing out of a growing desire to know God better. It is my prayer that we all catch the vision and have the desire to know God fully as He reveals Himself to us. Lord, as we look into Your holiness, the things of this world fade away into shadows in the light of You!

Prayer for life with a purpose,
the right purpose:

Father, help me to see and know I was created by You and for You, that I may know my chief end is to glorify You. Help me to see You in Your Word and come to a progressively deeper and sweeter knowledge of You. May all the rest of the world become a shadow in the light of knowing and loving You. May I come to You now, Lord, yielding my life to You, surrendering myself to You, not being shaped by the world but being transformed in my mind by You, Lord. I pray this in Jesus' name.

Amen.

Chapter 4

Who God Is in Himself

GOD KNOWS YOU, AND HE wants each of us to know Him. God reveals Himself to us in a number of ways—through His Word, through prayer, through the Body of Christ (all believers), through worship, and through creation itself; so we can absolutely know God.[11] The Apostle Paul described how God reveals Himself in creation:

> [19] For what can be known about God is plain to them, because God has shown it to them. [20] For his invisible attributes, namely, his eternal power and divine nature, have been clearly perceived, ever since the creation of the world, in the things that have been made. So they are without excuse.
>
> *(Romans 1:19-20)*

One of the best ways to know God is simply to read and think on what He has said about Himself. God has shown us and told us who He is through His Word, the

Holy Bible. He is the best source of knowledge about Himself, and so we must spend time with Him and listen to God as He speaks to us in and through the very Word of God, the Holy Bible. Often people say, "I just have trouble finding time to read the Bible." Here is a simple but pointed observation: Reading the Bible is not a matter of finding time but establishing priorities. If God is your number one priority in life, you have no problem finding time to listen to what He has to say. We need to seek God first before anything or anyone else.

Here a list of what God says or reveals about Himself,[12] what many have referred to as the "attributes of God." In the English Standard Version of the Holy Bible, quoted above, Romans 1:19-20 refers to God's "invisible attributes" and "divine nature." There are many books and other writings listing the attributes of God that include attributes beyond those I have chosen to list here. There are also some very scholarly writings that have a shorter list than the ones listed here. The attributes of God presented here seem to be both clear and sufficient. The ones that might be added to this list are, in my observation, simply part and parcel of what is listed here. For example, some would list "good" as an attribute, and certainly God is absolutely good in every way; however, the holiness and fairness of God incorporate His goodness. The simple truth is that all of God's attributes are complementary and supportive of one another. There are no inconsistencies of any kind in God. So, the list of God's attributes offered here includes the following:

- God is One: Father, Son, and Holy Spirit.
- God is light.
- God is love.
- God is infinite.

- God is eternal.
- God is almighty.
- God is all knowing.
- God is omnipresent.
- God is merciful.
- God is just.
- God is gracious.
- God is sovereign.
- God is unchanging.
- God is holy.
- God is fair.
- God is righteous.

These attributes ("divine qualities") of God reveal all we need to know about God in order to love and trust and worship and live for Him. No matter how long a list we might choose to give, we know God is so much more than these simple words and more than all the words this world contains. God cannot be defined with a pen or a word processor; God is infinitely larger than even our deepest sense and knowledge of who He is.

We have to be careful when we describe God. One of the problems is that we tend to speak of God using the same words and phrases we might use for other people. When we are describing people, we speak of their personality traits, how they act. This may be an acceptable means of describing people, but it does not work for God at all. When we speak of the attributes of God, we are not speaking of how God acts but of what and who God is.

God does not act lovingly; God is love! God does not simply extend grace; He is gracious. God is holy. When we read, "God is light," it is not just a description of what God has done but of who God is. God is light; light is part of God's essence. This is true of all God's attributes. These attributes are who God is, and so when we come to know God, we are coming to know He is light, love, grace, and likewise for each of God's limitless attributes.

God's attributes do not change depending upon the circumstances He is confronted with. God is not a loving God on certain days and a just God on other days. God is loving and just at the same time, all the time. In fact, all of God's attributes work perfectly and seamlessly together at all times. God's holiness is in perfect step with His graciousness. God's perfect knowledge of all things is completely in line with His mercy.

We need to know God because He is God. We need to know God because He is our Creator, our Savior, and our Strength; He is our everything. We also need to know God because knowing God as He really is will guide us through the troubled waters we encounter daily. When we know God loves us, know He isn't going anywhere, know He never changes, and know He is fair in every way, we will be transformed in how we see and respond to life's challenges.

Knowing God gives you real confidence to face the storm that will come blowing into your life today. Knowing God doesn't just guide us through the storm but allows us to dance in the rain with great peace and joy. We have new strength to face life.

> [10] for the joy of the LORD is your strength.
> *(Nehemiah 8:10)*

Oh the joy that daily floods the soul of the one who leans upon the everlasting Lord. Life really begins when you are fully trusting in the one true God and nothing that life throws at you can take that joy from you. One may, as I did earlier today, lose sight of this truth momentarily, but the minute we bring ourselves back[13] into the presence of God, the joy of who He is carries us through.

> [4] Rejoice in the Lord always; again I will say, rejoice. [5] Let your reasonableness be known to everyone. The Lord is at hand; [6] do not be anxious about anything, but in everything by prayer and supplication with thanksgiving let your requests be made known to God. [7] And the peace of God, which surpasses all understanding, will guard your hearts and your minds in Christ Jesus.
>
> *(Philippians 4:4-7)*

Prayer to see and begin to better understand the reality and daily significance to each of us of who God is, His divine attributes:

God, thank You that You are light for our eyes and our feet as we trod the paths of life; You are love that we might love You and others; thank You that You are infinite in all Your ways; You are eternal and invite us into eternal life; You are almighty in the time of our needs; You are all knowing when we don't know up from down; You are present when we feel so alone; You are merciful every morning without measure; You are just in all You do, fair in every way; Your grace is sufficient for us; You are sovereign over all; You are holy and call us to be holy. Thank You, Father, Son, and Holy Spirit, that You are all of these and infinitely more, and all of these things You are, You have always been and shall ever be—You change not. Thank You, Lord.

Amen.

Chapter 5

God Is One: Father, Son, and Holy Spirit

⁴ "Hear, O Israel: The LORD our God, the LORD is one.

(Deuteronomy 6:4)

THE HOLY TRINITY IS ONE God who exists in three persons—Father, Son, and Holy Spirit—who are one. The absolute truth of the Trinity is simultaneously undeniable yet wholly unexplainable with words. The inexplicable complexity of the Trinity does not speak against its reality but instead stands strongly supportive of the Trinity. God is far above knowing. He reveals Himself perfectly according to His will, and His revelation is more than sufficient in every way. Yet in God's oneness and in His Trinitarianism, we can only say, "Thou knowest, O Lord."

The Holy Trinity is clearly presented from Genesis to Revelation. The existence of the Trinity, while vigorously disputed by a relatively small group of professing Christians, has been fully recognized by the vast majority of Christianity since shortly after the death of Christ Jesus.

This is not an explanation of the incomprehensible mystery of the truth and holiness of the Trinity. The existence of the Trinity (Father, Son, and Holy Spirit) is abundantly clear in Scripture. Believing in and trusting God are foundational to Christianity. Think of Abram (later to be renamed Abraham), who believed God against all odds (his age about one hundred, his wife barren and about age ninety) that he would become the father of a son and of many nations. Faith in God is required, but the reality is that everyone has faith in one thing or another. The fact that the Trinity cannot be fully explained or understood does not stand in opposition to the reality of the Trinity. The Trinity will never be reasoned out; it is perceived by faith in God as He reveals the reality to us throughout the whole of Scripture.

The existence and reality of the Trinity are mysterious yet imminently apparent in the Word of God. Beyond the Word of God, the personal experience of relationship with the Father through the Son as guided and filled by the Holy Spirit is all the evidence needed for personal witness. Instead of weighing against its own reality, the incomprehensibility of the Trinity is a strong confirmation to all who seek God by faith. God has given us more than sufficient evidence for all we need to know of Him, but He would not be the one true God if He could be contained within or explained by the human mind. We, you and I, the creation, cannot fully comprehend the Creator! If we could fully understand God, He would not in fact be God.

The Triune God — Father, Son, and Holy Spirit (someone has said the three "Whos" of the one "What"[14]) — is present and evident in God's Word from Genesis to Revelation. In the same way that God as Father, Son, and Holy Spirit is evident throughout Scripture, He is likewise fully evident experientially in the daily life of a born-again, Spirit-filled Christ follower. Yet our experience falls far short of a full experience or explanation of Almighty God.

God, who is above our ability to fully comprehend, has nonetheless revealed Himself in His Word, in personal experiences with all who are in Christ, and in His own creation. We have been presented with more than enough God for us to see Him and know Him. Yet, there is much more to God than we will ever take in. Nowhere is that more true than when we look at the Triune God.

The Triune God has always been. God the Father, God the Son, and God the Holy Spirit—not three Gods; there is only one God, but He is one God existing in three persons—has always been and so shall He always be. In John 17:24 Jesus spoke of the love of the Father for the Son before the foundation of the world.

> [24]Father, I desire that they also, whom you have given me, may be with me where I am, to see my glory that you have given me because you loved me before the foundation of the world.
>
> *(John 17:24)*

In our humanity, we are presently limited by the dimensions of time, space, and matter. Because our whole frame of reference is with what can be held in our hand, grasping the full reality of what exists beyond the physical is impossible apart from faith. Yet, as challenging as the Trinity is to understand, a born-again Christian experientially knows the Trinity in their heart and spirit because the Trinity is a part of our daily experience of God.

God knows more about God than any person ever has known or could know. There is no better resource for knowing God than the Word of God. Let us see what God Himself reveals about Father, Son, and Holy Spirit in the Bible. First, let's look at Genesis:

> [1] In the beginning, God created the heavens and the earth. [2] The earth was without form and void, and darkness was over the face of the deep. And the Spirit of God was hovering over the face of the waters.
>
> [3] And God said, "Let there be light," and there was light. [4] And God saw that the light was good. And God separated the light from the darkness. [5] God called the light Day, and the darkness he called Night. And there was evening and there was morning, the first day.
>
> *(Genesis 1:1-5)*

Here in Genesis, we see Father God as Creator. Simultaneously, we see the Holy Spirit—"Spirit of God"—present "hovering over the face of the waters." Then God speaks and light is created. We know from John's Gospel, chapter 1 and verse 1, that "In the beginning was the Word," and that refers to Jesus. Jesus is the "Word" who is the agent of creation referred to in Genesis. So in creation, we see the one God who is Father, Son, and Holy Spirit.

Later in Genesis, we see God referring to Himself in this way:

> [26] Then God said, "Let us make man in our image, after our likeness. And let them have dominion over the fish of the sea and over the birds of the heavens and over the livestock and over all the earth and over every creeping thing that creeps on the earth."
>
> *(Genesis 1:26)*

^{22} Then the LORD God said, "Behold, the man has become like one of us in knowing good and evil."

(Genesis 3:22)

^{7} Come, let us go down and there confuse their language, so that they may not understand one another's speech."

(Genesis 11:7)

Love stands as both abstract and concrete proof of the Holy Trinity. We know from Scripture and from experience that God is love.

^{8} Anyone who does not love does not know God, because God is love.

(1 John 4:8)

Because we know God is love and we know God never changes, we are led to the unavoidable conclusion that love existed prior to creation. Love, to exist, must have the one loving and the one being loved. Prior to creation, there existed God the Father loving God the Son, God the Son loving God the Holy Spirit, and God the Holy Spirit loving God the Father. The Trinity is self-evident in this one thing, that God has always been love and that love could only exist, prior to creation, in the three: Father, Son, and Holy Spirit.

One profound scriptural presentation of the Trinity is found in Matthew's Gospel:

^{13} Then Jesus came from Galilee to the Jordan to John, to be baptized by him. ^{14} John would have prevented him, saying, "I need to be baptized by you, and do you come to me?" ^{15} But Jesus answered him, "Let it be so now, for thus

it is fitting for us to fulfill all righteousness."
Then he consented. [16] And when Jesus was baptized, immediately he went up from the water,
and behold, the heavens were opened to him,
and he saw the Spirit of God descending like a
dove and coming to rest on him; [17] and behold,
a voice from heaven said, "This is my beloved
Son, with whom I am well pleased."

(Matthew 3:13-17)

Here we see that all three persons of the Trinity are
one God in triune appearance: Father in heaven, Son
coming up out of the water, and Holy Spirit descending upon Jesus.

A. W. Tozer gave us this observation on the Trinity:

Some persons who reject all they cannot explain have denied that God is a Trinity. Subjecting
the Most High to their cold, level-eyed scrutiny,
they conclude that it is impossible that He could
be both One and Three. These forget that their
whole life is enshrouded in mystery. They fail
to consider that any real explanation of even the
simplest phenomenon in nature lies hidden in
obscurity and can no more be explained than
can the mystery of the Godhead. . . .

The doctrine of the Trinity is truth for the heart.
The spirit of man alone can enter through the veil
and penetrate into that Holy of Holies. "Let me
seek Thee in longing," pleaded Anselm,[15] "let me
long for Thee in seeking; let me find Thee in love,
and love Thee in finding." Love and faith are at
home in the mystery of the Godhead. Let reason
kneel in reverence outside.[16]

Christ did not hesitate to use the plural form when
speaking of Himself along with the Father and the Spirit.

[23] We will come to him and make our home with him.

(John 14:23)

Yet again He said,

[30] I and the Father are one.

(John 10:30)

A. W. Tozer said, "It is most important that we think of God as Trinity in Unity, neither confounding the Persons nor dividing the Substance. Only so may we think rightly of God and in a manner worthy of Him and of our own souls."[17]

It was our Lord's claim to equality with the Father that outraged the religionists of His day and led at last to His crucifixion. The attack on the doctrine of the Trinity two centuries later by Arius and others was also aimed at Christ's claim to deity. During the Arian controversy, 318 church fathers (many of them maimed and scarred by the physical violence suffered in earlier persecutions) met at Nicaea and adopted a statement of faith, one section of which runs,

I believe in one Lord Jesus Christ,
the Only Begotten Son of God,
born of the Father before all ages,
God from God, Light from Light,
true God from true God,
begotten, not made, consubstantial with the Father,
through him all things were made.[18]

For more than sixteen hundred years, this has stood as the final test of orthodoxy, as well it should, for it condenses in theological language the teaching of the New Testament concerning the position of the Son in the Godhead.

The Nicene Creed also pays tribute to the Holy Spirit as being Himself God and equal to the Father and the Son:

> *I believe in the Holy Spirit, the Lord, the giver of life,*
> *who proceeds from the Father and the Son,*
> *who with the Father and Son is adored and glorified.*[19]

God as Father, Son, and Holy Spirit is and has always been. They have no cause, no origin. God has always been. He told Moses His name is "I AM WHO I AM" (Exodus 3:14). In the Gospel of John we read,

> [58] Jesus said to them, "Truly, truly, I say to you, before Abraham was, I am."
>
> *(John 8:58)*

Then, regarding the Holy Spirit we see in Genesis, chapter 1:

> [2] The earth was without form and void, and darkness was over the face of the deep. And the Spirit of God was hovering over the face of the waters.
>
> *(Genesis 1:2)*

God is and has always been:

> [1] Lord, you have been our dwelling place
> in all generations.

> [2] *Before the mountains were brought forth,*
> *or ever you had formed the earth and the world,*
> *from everlasting to everlasting you are God.*
>
> *(Psalm 90:1-2)*

We see from John's First Epistle a picture of Father, Son, and Holy Spirit:

> [9] In this the love of God was made manifest among us, that God sent his only Son into the world, so that we might live through him. [10] In this is love, not that we have loved God but that he loved us and sent his Son to be the propitiation for our sins. [11] Beloved, if God so loved us, we also ought to love one another. [12] No one has ever seen God; if we love one another, God abides in us and his love is perfected in us.
> [13] By this we know that we abide in him and he in us, because he has given us of his Spirit. [14] And we have seen and testify that the Father has sent his Son to be the Savior of the world. [15] Whoever confesses that Jesus is the Son of God, God abides in him, and he in God.
>
> *(1 John 4:9-15)*

What does the Trinity mean to me and to you today? Everything! God the Father has created us to be in relationship with Him. God the Son died that we might be reconciled to God the Father; and Jesus is before God right now as our advocate, pleading our case before the Father. Jesus sent the Holy Spirit to guide us into all truth. Listen to what Jesus Himself said about the Holy Spirit:

> [4] And while staying with them he ordered them not to depart from Jerusalem, but to wait for the promise of the Father, which, he said, "you heard from me; [5] for John baptized with water, but you will be baptized with the Holy Spirit not many days from now."
>
> *(Acts 1:4-5)*

Yes, we can see the Holy Trinity, but we still must acknowledge there is much about God that cannot be known to man. God is so much larger than man can ever possibly understand.

> *[8] For my thoughts are not your thoughts,*
> *neither are your ways my ways, declares the LORD.*

> *[9] For as the heavens are higher than the earth,*
> *so are my ways higher than your ways*
> *and my thoughts than your thoughts.*
> *(Isaiah 55:8-9)*

What we do know of the Trinity we know by faith and by experience. I may not be able to tell you so much about the Trinity in a scholarly sense, yet I can give you a strong witness from my own experience. God is more real than anything I can put my hand on, see with my eyes, or sense with any other sense. The God of the Bible, existing as Father, Son, and Holy Spirit, ministers to me and in me and, I pray, through me daily. Nothing in this temporary world is as real as the everlasting reality of God the Father, Son, and Holy Spirit.

Let me close this chapter with one other quote from A. W. Tozer:

Who is this within the veil who dwells in fiery manifestations? It is none other than God Himself, "One God the Father Almighty, Maker of heaven and earth, and of all things visible and invisible," and "One Lord Jesus Christ, the only begotten Son of God; begotten of His Father before all worlds, God of God, Light of Light, Very God of Very God; begotten, not made; being of one substance with the Father," and "the Holy Ghost, the Lord and Giver of life, Who proceedeth from the Father and the Son, Who with the Father and the Son together is worshipped and glorified." Yet this holy Trinity is One God, for "we worship one God in Trinity, and Trinity in Unity; neither confounding the Persons, nor dividing the Substance. For there is one Person of the Father, another of the Son, and another of the Holy Ghost. But the Godhead of the Father, of the Son, and of the Holy Ghost, is all one: the glory equal and the majesty coeternaI." So in part run the ancient creeds, and so the inspired Word declares.[20]

Prayer acknowledging God as Father, Son, and Holy Spirit:

Father, Son, and Holy Spirit, we acknowledge right now that You and You alone are God. You are one, dwelling in perfect unity since before time, from all eternity. We don't fully understand the Godhead, but we know that Father, Son, and Holy Spirit are each and all fully one and yet each operate in different but completely harmonious ways to bring us to a saving knowledge of Christ, saving us and leading us and sustaining us and keeping us and carrying us through this life into life eternal. We thank You, God, for loving us in the unique ways that only You can, ever have, and ever will. You are God, and our everything is in You. Lord, help us to be one with You as You—Father, Son, and Holy Spirit—are and have always been one.

Amen.

Chapter 6

God Is Light

> [5] This is the message we have heard from him and proclaim to you, that God is light, and in him is no darkness at all.
>
> *(1 John 1:5)*

GOD IS THE BLESSED LIGHT to show the way, and He is the Way. "God is light" is not a message about what God does but who God is. "God is light!" There is no darkness in God. We never have to worry that God is going to have a bad day; He is always light. It is who God is. He is the light that never goes out, never dims or fades.

What does "God is light" mean to me personally? If I want light, I can just get up and flip the switch myself, right? Yes, unless you lose power, you can get up and flip a switch and there is light, but this is only true because God is light and apart from Him there would be no light of any kind. He is light and the source of all light (not Thomas Edison and not the power company); all light is ultimately from God.

> [1] In the beginning, God created the heavens and the earth. [2] The earth was without form

and void, and darkness was over the face of the deep. And the Spirit of God was hovering over the face of the waters.

3 And God said, "Let there be light," and there was light. 4 And God saw that the light was good. And God separated the light from the darkness. 5 God called the light Day, and the darkness he called Night. And there was evening and there was morning, the first day.

(Genesis 1:1-5)

He is not *the* light, He is not *a* light, He is light.[21]God's nature is light. God is not just light but He is also the source of light, and it was His very first act in creation. He spoke and there was light.

God is light "and in him is no darkness at all" means there are not even shadows with God. He is perfect, pure light. There is not even a hint of shadow or darkness. Light does not fellowship with darkness; the two are opposing forces. Light conquers darkness. This is important for us to know on several levels; the one I want to focus on is our thoughts of "little sins."

God knows of no such thing as a "little sin"; sin is absolutely putrid to God, offensive to Him in every way. There is no such thing as a "little white lie." Lying is contrary to God, and He hates it in me, in you, or in anyone. We need to know God is light and in Him there is not even a shadow of darkness. This principle of absolute light extends to all things: there is no such thing as an innocent look at a pornographic website; there is no such thing as covering something little up; there is no such thing as harmless gossip; and on and on. God is light; in Him is *no darkness at all!*

When you are born again and God is living in you, then the light in you is greater than the darkness around you!

⁴ But you belong to God, my dear children. You have already won a victory over those people, because the Spirit who lives in you is greater than the spirit who lives in the world.

(1 John 4:4, NLT)

We need to know the light in us is greater than the darkness around us. We will talk about God's power more specifically in a later chapter, but "God is light" speaks of a great power to overcome darkness. We need to walk each day with a clear awareness that the power of God exhibited in His light is with us and in us and is able to and has already overcome the darkness that comes against us.

What does "God is light" have to do with our daily lives? How will knowing God is light and in Him is no darkness at all help me pay my bills, cure my cancer, solve my marriage issues? When we know and embrace the truth that God is light and in Him there is no darkness, it will transform our lives as we live each day in the pure light of this great truth of who God is. We live and face our challenges in the pure light of God; it is who He is. The cancer diagnosis is brought into the light, and we know our loving God is in control. No matter what a test result shows, in God all is well. The same can be said for each of these daily issues that most of us face on a regular basis. Start looking at life from the standpoint of being loved by the one true God, who is perfect light.

Darkness confronts us daily. Darkness comes in the form of evil thoughts that beset each of us—about other people, about our circumstances, about who we are. When we know God is light and we, in faith, walk in that light, the darkness is driven back by the light. Light in us (God) reveals the sin of attacking others; the truth about whose we are and that He is bigger than our circumstances; that we are new creations in Christ, the old has gone and all things have been made new. We can say assuredly God is light; He is in my life; no matter what dark clouds appear in this world today, with God I am okay. The light of God in me and in you is greater than any darkness that exists.

God is light, a light that outshines the darkness of "you have cancer," "I am leaving you," "you are no good," "you have no money," or any other circumstance that confronts you today. In the popular vernacular one might ask, "What is in your wallet?" If your answer is "God is in my life, and I am in God," then you are dwelling in light—and not just any light but *the* light—and in Him there is no darkness. No one can say or do anything to force us into darkness. All born-again Christians can say with total assurance, "By the grace of God, I am in the light; all is well."

Light is good. In every aspect in our life, we sense and know that light is good. Light speaks of good, and even more, light is a good that seeks to spread— sending forth its wonderful qualities that bring good things to everything touched by them. Think of how wonderful the light is when you see the first gleam of daybreak. The dark night is dispelled with the first hint of dawn. That is all about light. God is light.

When people want to do bad things, they seek to hide it in the darkness. If you want to expose evil, you bring the light to shine on it. We all—yes, all of us— have things we wish and hope the light never shines on. The truth is, even in those challenging circumstances, the best thing that can happen is for light to come in. Once we confess our darkness to God, we have more light and less shadow.

¹⁶ Do not be deceived, my beloved brothers. ¹⁷ Every good gift and every perfect gift is from above, coming down from the Father of lights with whom there is no variation or shadow due to change. ¹⁸ Of his own will he brought us forth by the word of truth, that we should be a kind of firstfruits of his creatures.

(James 1:16-18)

In God there is no darkness or even any shadows. God's presence and purpose in our lives bring us into His light and allow us to see all the darkness disappear. In God—not just His presence but God in us—there can be no shadows. The light is good. When we learn of God's nature, that He is light, it frees us to confess our sins, shed the darkness and the shadows, and live in the pure light of His love— His "Son-Light." The light of God in our lives signifies that which is really good, eternally good; all darkness is driven away.

The light of God in my life reveals areas of darkness in me. One of these will prevail: either I will offer my dark spot to the light (confess and repent) or I will turn to darkness and break my fellowship with God. Light and dark have no communion. God is light, and He makes all the difference in our lives and in this world in which we live.

A commentary on 1 John describes the light of God this way: "The Divine Light is subject to no spots, no eclipse, no twilight, no night; as a Source of light it cannot in any degree fail."[22] We are called to the light, to "walk in the light":

⁶ If we say we have fellowship with him while we walk in darkness, we lie and do not practice the truth. ⁷ But if we walk in the light,

as he is in the light, we have fellowship with one another, and the blood of Jesus his Son cleanses us from all sin.

(1 John 1:6-7)

We will also see, because of God's other attributes, the light is not going away; it is forever and ever, and as we come to know God better, His light grows brighter day by day. Come, Lord Jesus, and let the light of Your love shine into the darkness of this world and into our very lives.

Prayer for the light of God in our lives:

God, You are the light, and we ask You to shine Your light into our lives right now. Reveal to us any shadows or darkness that we are trying to hold on to, and dispel the evil through Your presence in us as we acknowledge and confess our sins and turn from darkness to You. Lord, help us to know that no matter how dark our circumstances may seem, You are light, and when our circumstances are exposed to You, darkness, no matter how dark the dark, disappears. In You there is no darkness at all. By putting our trust in You, the darkness disappears from our lives. Your light far outshines and dispels the darkness. We thank You, Lord, that whether our problems go away or You work through them, we rejoice because the darkness is gone. We know no matter how difficult the problem, You are brighter than the darkest dark and the evil must flee in Your presence. Thank You, God, that You are light and in You, and You in us, there is no darkness at all.

Amen.

Chapter 7

God Is Love

> ⁸ Anyone who does not love does not know God, because God is love.
>
> *(1 John 4:8)*

THE MESSAGE HERE IS CLEAR: Love is the very essence of what God is. Theologian Adam Clarke put it so well when he said,

> It has been well observed that, although God is holy, just, righteous, etc., he is never called *holiness*, *justice*, etc., in the *abstract*, as he is here called LOVE. This seems to be the essence of the Divine nature, and all other attributes to be only modifications of this.[23]

Love is a challenging word in English because we use the one word to express how we feel about food, cars, favorite sports teams, people, and God. In the New Testament, there are four distinct Greek words for love, each referring to different types of love. The word referenced above in 1 John 4:8 ("God is love") is the word *agape*.

Agape is:

> Love, affectionate regard, goodwill, benevo-
> lence. With reference to God's love, it is God's
> willful direction toward man. It involves God do-
> ing what He knows is best for man and not neces-
> sarily what man desires. For example, John 3:16
> states, "For God so loved [ēgápēsen] the world,
> that he gave." What did He give? Not what man
> wanted, but what God knew man needed, i.e.,
> His Son to bring forgiveness to man.[24]

When God *agapes* us, it means He is doing that which
is the very best for us. What God seeks is better than anything else we could ever find or do on our own. The only
way we miss the very best in life is if we miss God because God always comes with our best as He *agapes* us.

When God speaks of love, it has nothing to do with
emotion. God is referring to His intentional and purposeful will of bringing us what is best for us. God's love
is seen in both who He is and what He does. Nowhere is
this more obvious than in this familiar verse:

> [16] For God so loved the world, that he gave
> his only Son, that whoever believes in him
> should not perish but have eternal life.
>
> *(John 3:16)*

God's love for us is us getting the very best He has
for us. Knowing God's love is best and trusting God in
His love are essential for our spiritual growth. Receive
and rest on this truth: In every way and at all times
God expresses Himself in love to us. Love is such a
pervasive and intrinsic aspect of who God is and all
He does; it is imperative we understand these very
pointed statements about God's love and our responsibility in responding to His love.

⁸ Anyone who does not love does not know God, because God is love.

(1 John 4:8)

¹⁶ For this is how God loved the world: He gave his one and only Son, so that everyone who believes in him will not perish but have eternal life. ¹⁷ God sent his Son into the world not to judge the world, but to save the world through him.

(John 3:16-17, NLT)

¹⁰ In this is love, not that we have loved God but that he loved us and sent his Son to be the propitiation for our sins. ¹¹ Beloved, if God so loved us, we also ought to love one another. ¹² No one has ever seen God; if we love one another, God abides in us and his love is perfected in us.

(1 John 4:10-12)

God is love, and He calls us into a love relationship with Him. God calls you and me to love. Jesus expressed the centrality of love in the life of a Christian during His conversation with an expert in the religious law:

³⁶ "Teacher, which is the most important commandment in the law of Moses?"

³⁷ Jesus replied, "'You must love the LORD your God with all your heart, all your soul, and all your mind.' ³⁸ This is the first and greatest commandment. ³⁹ A second is equally important: 'Love your neighbor as yourself.' ⁴⁰ The entire law and all the demands of the prophets are based on these two commandments."

(Matthew 22:36-40, NLT)

The call to love is powerful and should penetrate and permeate every aspect of a Christian's life. There is no way to avoid God's call to love Him by obeying His command to love others.

> ¹⁵If you love me, you will keep my commandments.
>
> *(John 14:15)*

> ²⁰ If anyone says, "I love God," and hates his brother, he is a liar; for he who does not love his brother whom he has seen cannot love God whom he has not seen. ²¹ And this command-ment we have from him: whoever loves God must also love his brother.
>
> *(1 John 4:20-21)*

God is love; we are not. Following God's lead here is not our natural human response to life and people. We do not know how to *agape* with our flesh. This is why Jesus told Nicodemus we must be born again not of the flesh but of the Spirit.

> ³ Jesus answered him, "Truly, truly, I say to you, unless one is born again he cannot see the kingdom of God." ⁴ Nicodemus said to him, "How can a man be born when he is old? Can he enter a second time into his mother's womb and be born?" ⁵ Jesus answered, "Truly, truly, I say to you, unless one is born of water and the Spirit, he cannot enter the kingdom of God. ⁶ That which is born of the flesh is flesh, and that which is born of the Spirit is spirit.
>
> *(John 3:3-6)*

If a person's life is characterized by love, we can know for sure it is the presence of the Holy Spirit who accomplishes in us that which God has called us to.

> [14] For the love of Christ controls us, because we have concluded this: that one has died for all, therefore all have died; [15] and he died for all, that those who live might no longer live for themselves but for him who for their sake died and was raised.
>
> [16] From now on, therefore, we regard no one according to the flesh. Even though we once regarded Christ according to the flesh, we regard him thus no longer. [17] Therefore, if anyone is in Christ, he is a new creation. The old has passed away; behold, the new has come.
>
> *(2 Corinthians 5:14-17)*

Daily living out the love God calls us to is an act of the Holy Spirit in us. Even though we are new creatures, we are still residing in our earthly bodies, which we call flesh, and our flesh is at war with the Spirit in us. In order to live a life of love, we have to live by the Spirit not by the flesh.

> [16] But I say, walk by the Spirit, and you will not gratify the desires of the flesh. [17] For the desires of the flesh are against the Spirit, and the desires of the Spirit are against the flesh, for these are opposed to each other, to keep you from doing the things you want to do. [18] But if you are led by the Spirit, you are not under the law. [19] Now the works of the flesh are evident: sexual immorality, impurity, sensuality, [20] idolatry, sorcery, enmity, strife, jealousy, fits of anger, rivalries, dissensions, divisions,

[21] envy, drunkenness, orgies, and things like these. I warn you, as I warned you before, that those who do such things will not inherit the kingdom of God. [22] But the fruit of the Spirit is love, joy, peace, patience, kindness, goodness, faithfulness, [23] gentleness, self-control; against such things there is no law. [24] And those who belong to Christ Jesus have crucified the flesh with its passions and desires.

(Galatians 5:16-24)

The Holy Spirit in us is God in us, and God is love! For us to live out the love of God, we have to be obedient to the Spirit of God.

How does God's love change who we are and how we live? In everything and in every way! One way is this: How should we respond to mistreatment by others?[25] God is love and God is in control,[26] so whatever happens in our lives happens through the filter of God's love. When someone steps on our toes or confronts us head-on, we have to, in the Spirit, acknowledge that God is love and respond accordingly. I have to do some serious self-talking, which goes something like this:

> I want to give him a piece of my mind for what he said to or about me. But I know God is love, so what must I do?

> Let me walk through this truth about God:

> God is God.

> God is sovereign. (He has ultimate control and say-so over life.)

> God is love.

Whatever happens in my life is caused or allowed by God.

The events of my life are an expression of God's love.

I can rejoice in the Lord in what is happening; yes, even when it hurts, I can rejoice in the Lord because He is allowing this for His good purposes.

So, I can't give him a piece of my mind; instead, I have to *agape* him as God *agapes* me.

Because God loves me, He allows things to happen in my life that will, regardless of how they feel at the moment, work for my ultimate good and God's ultimate glory. So, I can know God is doing good stuff, and I can rejoice even in the midst of a problem.

> [28] And we know that for those who love God all things work together for good, for those who are called according to his purpose. [29] For those whom he foreknew he also predestined to be conformed to the image of his Son, in order that he might be the firstborn among many brothers.
>
> *(Romans 8:28-29)*

God's ultimate purpose is that we become Christlike. Christlikeness happens in the crucible of false accusations and mistreatments, the daily fare Jesus dealt with. So, no matter what is going on, we can:

> [4] Rejoice in the Lord always; again I will say, rejoice.
>
> *(Philippians 4:4)*

The transformation from selfishness to Christlikeness happens in the storms of life. Knowing God loves us, knowing God desires the best for us, and knowing the storm clouds are a gift from God to take us from where we are to where we need to be allow us to embrace our sufferings as part of God's love. Paul recognized this and proclaimed the following as his great desire:

> [10] that I may know him and the power of his resurrection, and may share his sufferings, becoming like him in his death, [11] that by any means possible I may attain the resurrection from the dead.
>
> *(Philippians 3:10-11)*

> [20] But our citizenship is in heaven, and from it we await a Savior, the Lord Jesus Christ, [21] who will transform our lowly body to be like his glorious body, by the power that enables him even to subject all things to himself.
>
> *(Philippians 3:20-21)*

As we begin to understand God as love and what that means for our lives and the circumstances we face, we undergo a transformation process that radically changes how we respond to life. James clearly proclaimed our new way of responding to life and all its challenges:

> [2] Dear brothers and sisters, when troubles of any kind come your way, consider it an opportunity for great joy. [3] For you know that when your faith is tested, your endurance has a chance to grow. [4] So let it grow, for when your endurance is fully developed, you will be perfect and complete, needing nothing.
>
> *(James 1:2-4, NLT)*

The events of our lives are an expression of God's love. The love of God does not seek our approval but our transformation, our ultimate happiness. In this very hour, I find myself battling what seem to me to be false personal attacks. Let me translate that: God is trying to grow me up, but my pride is getting in the way. Pride is the very thing that has to depart for us to live a life in love; the love God has called us to by His acts of love in and toward us is a life of humility.

We have to learn to trust God with all our heart; we have to know God and live our lives with the clear knowledge that God is love and what He permits into our lives is an expression of His love. God is love, and the events of life are overlaid on and interlaced with God's love. Our growing awareness that life is acted out on the canvas of God's love gives us a completely new perspective about our daily challenges. When we wake up with a growing awareness of God's *agape* love seeking the very best for us, we experience a transformational shift in how we live.

One of the most amazing biblical examples of this principle is found in the story of Joseph. Joseph, the son of Jacob, was sold into slavery by his older brothers; he was falsely accused of attempted rape and thrown into prison; he provided great help to some powerful men, who then promptly forgot about Joseph and left him in prison for years. Then suddenly Joseph was let out of prison and became prime minister over all of Egypt. Later, his brothers came to him for food; when they realized the person who was in charge over all of Egypt was the very brother they had sold into slavery, they were terrified. Joseph simply said to them,

[19] Do not fear, for am I in the place of God?
[20] As for you, you meant evil against me, but

God meant it for good, to bring it about that many people should be kept alive, as they are today.

(Genesis 50:19-20)

God is love—not that we loved Him, but that He loved us and gave His Son for us. God's love, the essence of who He is, provides comfort no matter what challenges and difficulties we encounter on our daily journey through life; we can and must always say, "I know God is love, He loves me, all is well no matter what!"

Prayer of recognition and thanksgiving for God's love:

Heavenly Father, You are love, and we rest in Your love today. Father, no matter what anyone else says, no matter how anyone else feels about us or toward us, You love us. Love is who You are. Thank You that Your love does not come and go but is constant; Your love is unchanging and Your love will never be less than it is right now; there is nothing we can do to make You love us more because Your love is perfect, full, and ever present. Lord, help us to comprehend the vastness of Your love for us in Christ; no matter what we are facing today, we can rest in Your love, which is higher than our struggle, deeper than our hurt, wider than the attack we face, and longer than the problem we are wrestling with. God is love, and all of life changes when we know who You are. You are a good, good Father; You are perfect in all of Your ways, especially in Your love. We love You, Lord.

Amen.

Chapter 8

God Is Infinite

⁵Great is our Lord, and abundant in power;
his understanding is beyond measure.
(Psalm 147:5)

IN OCTOBER 1962, THE ENTIRE world was held captive by the Cuban Missile Crisis. "Would Nikita Khrushchev and Fidel Castro destroy the world by starting a nuclear war?" I was an eight-year-old living in the small town of Meadville, Mississippi, and the adult conversation was dominated by fear of a world-ending nuclear war. With sleep eluding me, I lay in bed pondering a question born out of the adult conversations I kept overhearing: "If they blow up the world with hydrogen bombs, what will be when the world is gone?" This perplexing thought remained with me long after the crisis passed. Today people have similar thoughts and fears with both nuclear and terrorist threats hanging over us. We can be consumed with fear, or we can seek the one true answer to world-ending threats.

There was only one answer in 1962, and there is only one answer in 2016: the one and only infinite God. The world had a definite starting point, and it has a definite ending point. Not so with God. He is infinite, without beginning and without end. This created world and all that is in it had a specific point of beginning. There will also be a specific point when this world, as we know it, will cease to exist. This is a finite world, but God is infinite.

The primary reason we do not get God's infiniteness is that everything we can see, touch, hear, and smell is created. Every physical thing has a beginning date and an expiration date; in other words, everything we see and touch is finite. We, too, in our flesh, are finite people living in a finite world, and we have no real concept of God's infinitude.

All created things have a creator. Not so the creator. He cannot both create and be created; at least He can't be both and be God. God, the Creator, has no beginning or end; in fact, He cannot have a beginning or an end—if He did, He would not be God. God has always been, so shall He always be. He is before all things and after all things. He is Alpha and Omega. God is, in His very essence, infinite.

Does God's infinitude mean anything to you personally? What does God's infiniteness have to do with how you will live your life today? Everything and in every way! There is no attribute of God more important to our daily lives than God's infinitude. There is only one who is infinite, and He is the one and only true God who was and is and is to come. He is the great "I AM."

People have always made gods for themselves out of stone, metal, wood, and other objects. People have made money their god, fame their god, and all sorts of other gods. None of this works; you and I know this because we have experienced it personally. Every one of us, in one way or another, has experienced the effect of making something a god in our lives; none of those things work, and none of them lasts. We can only find what we need in the one true God who is, in His very essence, infinite.

The second crucial thing for us to see and know from God's infinitude is this: God is infinite in all His ways. God is infinite in His being, and He is infinite in His love. God is infinite in every aspect of who He is, in all His actions, thoughts, and attributes. For example, God is infinitely good, which is infinitely important for me and for you!

God's infiniteness is relevant and critical to each of us in our daily lives because life has moments that are so overwhelming, they literally suck the breath of life out of everyone involved: the death of a child, a devastating earthquake, a Hurricane Katrina, 9/11. The events are so disturbing that life itself ceases to make sense. In those times, a finite god who can be fully known and understood by our limited minds has no chance to truly be God. Only an infinite God, a God who has infinite knowledge and power and love, can overshadow and begin to make sense and purpose out of such unsettling times in our lives. In those times we can cry out and say, "Lord, I don't understand, but I am so thankful that You do. You know the beginning from the end. You, O Lord, can make sense of this, and we just look to and rest in You. Thank You for being God in and through these times."

Man has been on the earth for thousands of years. The study and contemplation of the human body and mind have been underway throughout the history of humankind. Likewise, humans have gazed upon the solar system and all its components, seeking to understand how it all fits together. Only a truly infinite God—a God who is above and beyond all that we see and understand—could possibly give account for the complexity of the far reaches of space as well as our human bodies and all their internal systems. These things, despite all our advances in science, are yet today infinitely beyond our understanding! Thus is God in His infiniteness revealed.

Now, let's bring God's infinitude home to the immediate discussions taking place around our kitchen tables and see how it matters. When you wake up in the morning knowing that radical Islamic jihadists and other terrorists would rejoice to see you, your family, your state, and even your nation totally annihilated; when you know there are countries and groups who would like nothing better than to strike your country with a nuclear explosive; when you know that you have nothing to protect you from such cataclysmic events, you must have an infinite God.

Only an infinite God can answer and give comfort in the face of such horrific thoughts. The immensity of the evil planned against you daily can only be kept in perspective by knowing God is infinite. He is infinite in every way—infinite in His love, wisdom, power, strength, presence, and peace. God's will and plans are infinitely higher and stronger than anything planned against us. We can say to such persons and to whoever seeks to do us in, "You come against me with your hate, but I stand in the strength of the great and constant 'I AM,' the God who made you and me. I will not fear, and I will not run. God is infinitely greater than your threats against me." When we rise up and when we lie down, as we walk about this upside-down world today, we see our desperate need for a very real God who truly loves us with an immeasurable love— an infinite love.

God's infiniteness is what allows us to reach out to

someone who would seek to destroy us and say, "God has told me to love you, and I obey Him now. God has told me to forgive you for wanting me and my family and my entire nation to be annihilated. I forgive you now in the matchless and infinite name of Jesus Christ."

Prayer acknowledging God's infinitude:

Lord, we are so grateful that You are God and that there is no limit to Your presence, Your provision, Your protection, and Your power. We trust You, God, because You are infinitely larger than our worst fears and nothing is too difficult for You. We thank You, Lord, that Your peace, which passes our ability to understand, will guard our hearts and our minds in Christ Jesus, and nothing this finite world throws our way can change Your purposes. You alone are God! You are in control, and we put all our trust and all our hope in You. We draw all our peace, comfort, and joy from the only true God; You are infinite in all Your ways.

Amen.

Chapter 9

God Is Eternal

¹ Lord, you have been our dwelling place
throughout all generations.

² Before the mountains were born
or you brought forth the whole world,
from everlasting to everlasting you are God.
(Psalm 90:1-2, NIV)

BEFORE TIME BEGAN, GOD WAS. He told Moses that His name was "I AM" (Exodus 3:14). He also said He is the Alpha and Omega:

> ¹³ I am the Alpha and the Omega, the first and the last, the beginning and the end.
> *(Revelation 22:13)*

God is eternal. He was God before creation. He will be God after this world ceases to be. God is eternal, without beginning and without end.

Does God being eternal mean anything specifically to our individual lives, or is this just meaningless chatter (what someone has referred to as "metaphysical bric-a-brac")? The answer is simple but profound: God's eternality is not just important today; it is absolutely crucial to every aspect of our lives—now and forever.

What do we mean when we say eternal? First, because we exist in time and have no way to go outside the time we are in, we have to admit we don't fully understand what eternal means. But, having given that disclaimer, let's state what we do know.

- God is.
- God has always been.
- God will always be.
- There is no time or point before time began that God was not.
- There is no time or point after time ceases that God will not be God.
- God was, is, and shall ever be.

So what? So everything! God can only be God if He is eternal. If God is not eternal, then there would be a time when God was not. If ever there was a time when God was not, then He would not be God—God would be whoever or whatever existed when God was not God. God is God and always has been and shall forever be.

God's eternality is not something He accomplishes or does; God's eternality is an essential ingredient of who God is. There is no part of God or any of His attributes that is not eternal. Just as God is infinite in all His ways, so God is eternal in who He is and in all of His ways.

Space, time, and matter are the essential ingredients we relate to as human beings. We occupy space, we are in time, and our bodies constitute matter. Physically, we are bound by these (space, time, and matter). God is eternal: He does not occupy space (yet He fills all of the world); He exists outside the realm of time (the eternal now); He is not a part of matter (He is larger than anything we know or can imagine but cannot be touched in the sense of touching something physical or something made of matter). Those ingredients (space, time, matter) are acted upon by what we call laws of nature, such as gravity. Everything in our physical being is subject to those laws of nature; God is not.

God, not being bound by time, is in the eternal present. God, in one continuous view, is looking at creation, all of time, Christ's first coming, the future return of Christ Jesus—and they are all simultaneous[27] to God. To Him, these are all now; all things are before His eyes at one time. These points on the continuum of time, as we measure and try to understand it, are one for God.

I best try to assimilate this in my mind by thinking of time and eternity like this: A yardstick represents all of time; the left end of the yardstick represents the time of creation; the right end of the yardstick represents the return of Christ Jesus; and, finally, a point (it doesn't matter which point) along that line of time, whether at thirteen inches or thirty-five and three quarters of an inch, represents the present. God is holding the yardstick and is simultaneously looking at every point in time along the time line from creation to the end. God is also looking into eternity past and eternity future at the same time. God is outside of and not bound by time. God is eternal.

> [9] *Remember the former things, those of long ago;*
> *I am God, and there is no other;*
> *I am God, and there is none like me.*

¹⁰ I make known the end from the beginning,
from ancient times, what is still to come.

I say: "My purpose will stand,
and I will do all that I please."

(Isaiah 46:9-10, NIV)

Listen now to what the eternal God says to us about our lives; His precious words tell of how He created us and has known us from eternity:

¹ You have searched me, Lord,
and you know me.

² You know when I sit and when I rise;
you perceive my thoughts from afar.

³ You discern my going out and my lying down;
you are familiar with all my ways.

⁴ Before a word is on my tongue
you, Lord, know it completely.

⁵ You hem me in behind and before,
and you lay your hand upon me.

⁶ Such knowledge is too wonderful for me,
too lofty for me to attain.

⁷ Where can I go from your Spirit?
Where can I flee from your presence?

⁸ If I go up to the heavens, you are there;
if I make my bed in the depths, you are there.

[9] *If I rise on the wings of the dawn,*
if I settle on the far side of the sea,

[10] *even there your hand will guide me,*
your right hand will hold me fast.

[11] *If I say, "Surely the darkness will hide me*
and the light become night around me,"

[12] *even the darkness will not be dark to you;*
the night will shine like the day,
for darkness is as light to you.

[13] *For you created my inmost being;*
you knit me together in my mother's womb.

[14] *I praise you because I am*
fearfully and wonderfully made;
your works are wonderful,
I know that full well.

[15] *My frame was not hidden from you*
when I was made in the secret place,
when I was woven together in the depths of the earth.

[16] *Your eyes saw my unformed body;*
all the days ordained for me were written in your book
before one of them came to be.

[17] *How precious to me are your thoughts, God!*
How vast is the sum of them!

[18] *Were I to count them,*
they would outnumber the grains of sand —
when I awake, I am still with you.

(Psalm 139:1-18, NIV)

Because of God's eternality, He knows you completely. God knows your past; He knows your future. God knows your words before you speak them; He knows your thoughts before you think them; He knows your steps before you take them. These are things God knew before there was time. Now, if the one true, eternal God knows all these things about you, who is your best resource when you have a question about your life? Who should you consult when you don't understand why you do what you do; why you don't do the things you want to do? God is eternal. He made you and me, and His eternality is absolutely necessary for our daily lives and our peace of mind and heart.

God's eternality is the reason God can say with certainty:

> ¹¹ "For I know the plans I have for you," says the LORD. "They are plans for good and not for disaster, to give you a future and a hope. ¹² In those days when you pray, I will listen. ¹³ If you look for me wholeheartedly, you will find me. ¹⁴ I will be found by you," says the LORD.
> *(Jeremiah 29:11-14, NLT)*

God's eternality is why we can and should trust Him in every aspect of our lives, the reason we don't need to worry about tonight or tomorrow, the reason we can go boldly into the day and the night with great confidence. When we put our trust in God, we are trusting in and relying on a God who is eternally loving. He enjoys perfect knowledge of the future. We can and should absolutely trust God, who is in the present and in the future. He said it so simply:

> ⁵ *Trust in the LORD with all your heart;*
> *do not depend on your own understanding.*

> ⁶ *Seek his will in all you do,*
> *and he will show you which path to take.*

> *(Proverbs 3:5-6, NLT)*

Counting on God for all our tomorrows is obvious because God is not guessing about what will happen tomorrow; He is in tomorrow while holding our hand today. God's eternality is key to our journey and finding peace and joy in it. Because God is eternal, we can live our lives with purpose, passion, and joy. God is eternal!

Prayer and praise for God's eternality:

God, You have been our dwelling place in every generation; You have always been and so shall You ever be. When we start to worry about tomorrow, help us to remember You are already there, and where You are, there is an abundance of peace and order and light and everything good. When we are inclined to dwell on our regrets over yesterday, Lord, help us to remember that as we have confessed our sins to You, you have forgiven us and remember our sins no more. God, You are the God of all our yesterdays, all our todays, and all our tomorrows. We rest in You, the unchanging, eternal God who has made great and wonderful promises that You always keep. When we lie down and when we rise up, may it be with our eyes upon You—the one and only eternal God who loves us more than we love ourselves. We pray this in the eternal and matchless name of our Lord and Savior, Jesus Christ.

Amen.

Chapter 10

God Is Almighty

WITH OUR MOUTHS WE SING, "Our God is an awesome God, He reigns from heaven above with wisdom, power, and love,"[28] but what do our hearts say about the power of God? Before we go to bed at night, before we rise in the morning, we need to have it settled in our minds that God is omnipotent. There is great comfort and peace in knowing God is all powerful. Knowing you are loved and watched over by Almighty God, who is bigger and more powerful than anything this day can bring, is the source of true joy. When we lie down and when we rise up, we can have confidence that our God has all power—power infinitely greater than the end of the month, rejection by a spouse, the opinions of others, the destruction of cancer, the grip of addiction, and the plans of terrorist who want us dead. God is omnipotent, and His power is greater than all of life's fiery darts!

The absolute key to a great day is being known and loved by a great God who is almighty in every way. We need to say "good-bye" to fear and worry and say "good morning" to the Lord of all creation, Almighty God!

> ¹² *But the LORD made the earth by his power,*
> *and he preserves it by his wisdom.*
>
> *With his own understanding*
> *he stretched out the heavens.*
>
> ¹³ *When he speaks in the thunder,*
> *the heavens roar with rain.*
>
> *He causes the clouds to rise over the earth.*
> *He sends the lightning with the rain*
> *and releases the wind from his storehouses.*
> *(Jeremiah 10:12-13, NLT)*

Every one of us faces challenges on a daily basis. We have way more month than money, we have a diagnosis that Tylenol will not fix, a spouse who is bound and determined to bring this relationship to the ground, or a child who has wandered far away and we cannot find them. Life is overwhelming to each of us. We are all facing giants that we don't have an answer for, and we are saying to ourselves, "How do I get through this?" If you are facing giants in your life (if you aren't, get ready because they are headed to your house next), if life seems impossible, then we need a fresh knowledge of Almighty God, who specializes in the impossible!

> ²⁶ But Jesus looked at them and said, "With man this is impossible, but with God all things are possible."
>
> *(Matthew 19:26)*

We live in very challenging times, scary times to be alive on earth. Today is no different from earlier generations. People in every generation have faced challenges just as daunting as we face today. We tend to forget our history lessons and the truths of Scripture. Let's take a quick tour through history and be reminded of God's omnipotence—His unlimited power, Almighty God!

You know about David and Goliath, right? But do you know that David was no different from you. There was nothing super about David. He was not created on a back lot of Hollywood. David was a young boy raised on the farm. He could just as easily have been a young boy raised in a rough section of a large city. The simple truth is, David was just like us. We need to remind ourselves how this played out with David.

He was the younger brother. His father, Jesse, sent him to check on his older brothers who were off at war against the Philistines. They were serving in Saul's army. When David arrived, his brothers immediately began to bully and belittle him. Can't you just imagine how they felt: "We are soldiers, and here our little brother, the sheepherder, has been sent by our father to check on us." They were quite embarrassed, so they took out their frustrations on David.

When David arrived at the battlefront, he found the Israelites all hiding and he could not understand why. Then David saw the source of their great fear: a mighty Philistine warrior, almost ten feet tall, with a huge sword and armor. This one man was challenging the whole Israelite army. Goliath was standing in the open and roared at the Israelites, "Come out here, you wimps; if there is anybody who is not afraid of me, come out here and fight like a man. Quit hiding in the rocks, and come out and meet me man to man."

David knew God. God had delivered David from lions and bears and many other foes as David shepherded his father's sheep. David knew from personal experience how mighty and powerful God is, and he knew this Philistine soldier was nothing to God. David reminded his people just who God is:

[32] "Don't worry about this Philistine," David told Saul. "I'll go fight him!"

[33] "Don't be ridiculous!" Saul replied. "There's no way you can fight this Philistine and possibly win! You're only a boy, and he's been a man of war since his youth."

[34] But David persisted. "I have been taking care of my father's sheep and goats," he said. "When a lion or a bear comes to steal a lamb from the flock, [35] I go after it with a club and rescue the lamb from its mouth. If the animal turns on me, I catch it by the jaw and club it to death. [36] I have done this to both lions and bears, and I'll do it to this pagan Philistine, too, for he has defied the armies of the living God! [37] The LORD who rescued me from the claws of the lion and the bear will rescue me from this Philistine!"

(1 Samuel 17:32-37, NLT)

David had spent many nights facing ferocious animals that wanted to kill his father's sheep. David was just a boy, but he was a boy who knew Yahweh, the one true living God. David knew all things are possible when your hope rests on Almighty God.

[37] Saul finally consented. "All right, go ahead," he said. "And may the LORD be with you!" . . .

[40] [David] picked up five smooth stones from a stream and put them into his shepherd's bag.

Then, armed only with his shepherd's staff and sling, he started across the valley to fight the Philistine.

[41] Goliath walked out toward David with his shield bearer ahead of him, [42] sneering in contempt at this ruddy-faced boy. [43] "Am I a dog," he roared at David, "that you come at me with a stick?" And he cursed David by the names of his gods. [44] "Come over here, and I'll give your flesh to the birds and wild animals!" Goliath yelled.

[45] David replied to the Philistine, "You come to me with sword, spear, and javelin, but I come to you in the name of the LORD of Heaven's Armies—the God of the armies of Israel, whom you have defied. [46] Today the LORD will conquer you, and I will kill you and cut off your head. And then I will give the dead bodies of your men to the birds and wild animals, and the whole world will know that there is a God in Israel! [47] And everyone assembled here will know that the LORD rescues his people, but not with sword and spear. This is the LORD's battle, and he will give you to us!"

[48] As Goliath moved closer to attack, David quickly ran out to meet him. [49] Reaching into his shepherd's bag and taking out a stone, he hurled it with his sling and hit the Philistine in the forehead. The stone sank in, and Goliath stumbled and fell face down on the ground.

[50] So David triumphed over the Philistine with only a sling and a stone, for he had no sword. [51] Then David ran over and pulled Goliath's sword from its sheath. David used it to kill him and cut off his head.

(1 Samuel 17:37, 40-51, NLT)

If you have asked yourself who God is and have answered that He is the Lord, all loving, infinite, eternal, and all powerful, then you are ready to run toward your giant today, knowing that God is in control. He is more powerful than anything you face.

God is not just all powerful, but in Christ, the all-powerful God is fully in us. When we are in Christ, the same Christ (the Holy Spirit of Christ) who is very God of very God resides in us. Here is what God's presence in our lives means to us:

> ⁴ But you belong to God, my dear children. You have already won a victory over those people, because the Spirit who lives in you is greater than the spirit who lives in the world.
>
> *(1 John 4:4, NLT)*

Follow David's example and say to cancer, to debt, to marital issues, to struggles with a child, to someone who seeks to destroy you: "You come at me with this cancer, this financial matter, this marital challenge. You do not know who you are fooling with, dude. I belong to Yahweh. He is all powerful, He is infinite, He is eternal, and He loves me. In fact, He loves me so much that He has adopted me. He gave His own Son for me. So, you may look big, you may feel big, and you may be big by the way the world looks at things; but I am here to tell you, I don't see things as the world sees them. I have the power of God on my side, and today, not I but the Lord will conquer you. You are whipped!"

Whatever your circumstances today, the God who brought down the walls of Jericho with a shout, who parted the Red Sea and allowed His people to walk across on dry ground, who declared to Joshua, "Don't worry; I will be right there with you as you lead these million-plus difficult people," and to Stephen, "Don't let these people and their rocks scare you; I am God and beside Me there is no other," He is still God and He is still almighty in every way.

The God who made you and loves you and is with you is El Shaddai—God Almighty. I pray that God would give you and me this vision:

> [15] When the servant of the man of God rose early in the morning and went out, behold, an army with horses and chariots was all around the city. And the servant said, "Alas, my master! What shall we do?" [16] [Elisha] said, "Do not be afraid, for those who are with us are more than those who are with them." [17] Then Elisha prayed and said, "O LORD, please open his eyes that he may see." So the LORD opened the eyes of the young man, and he saw, and behold, the mountain was full of horses and chariots of fire all around Elisha.
>
> *(2 Kings 6:15-17)*

May God help us to know who He is. May we know that He who is in us is greater, stronger, and more powerful than he who is in the world. May our eyes be opened to know that the journey before us is one we don't take alone. We do not go out to face the giants today with only our slingshot but with the power of El Shaddai, God Almighty.

Prayer of thanksgiving and praise and trust in our Almighty God:

Father, we stand at peace in your presence. We fear nothing because You, the Lord our God, are with us; "your rod and your staff" comfort us (Psalm 23:4). As we face the giants in our lives today, we say, as David did, "You come against us with threats and disease and heartache, but we come against those threats not in our own strength but in the strength of Almighty God who was and is and is to come." We come into this day of challenges not fearing because greater is He who is in us than he who is in the world. You, O God, are infinitely greater than those things that threaten to take us down today. What a mighty God we serve! We will face this day not in our strength but in the strength of Almighty God.

Amen.

Chapter 11

God Is All Knowing

³³ Oh, the depth of the riches and wisdom and knowledge of God! How unsearchable are his judgments and how inscrutable his ways!
(Romans 11:33)

GOD IS OMNISCIENT; IF SOMETHING is knowable, God knows it. What a blessing it is that our God is so wise; in fact, He is the source and creator of all knowledge. There is no knowledge anywhere except that it arises from Him and is about Him.

¹⁰ The fear of the LORD is the beginning of wisdom, and the knowledge of the Holy One is insight.
(Proverbs 9:10)

⁵ Great is our Lord, and abundant in power; his understanding is beyond measure.
(Psalm 147:5)

²¹ For a man's ways are before the eyes of the LORD, and he ponders all his paths.
(Proverbs 5:21)

*² You know when I sit down and when I rise up;
you discern my thoughts from afar.*

*³ You search out my path and my lying down
and are acquainted with all my ways.*

*⁴ Even before a word is on my tongue,
behold, O LORD, you know it altogether.*

(Psalm 139:2-4)

The greatest and most powerful computers ever created are simple toys compared to the human brain. Despite all our technology, the intricacies of the human body are far beyond the understanding of medical science. God created the human body and the brain that directs and controls it; He spoke it all into existence. God is omniscient, and there is no limit to His knowledge.

What does it mean to us today that our God knows all things? God's perfect knowledge of all things is meaningful and practical to each of our lives right now. Begin with this thought: God knows you completely, much better than any parent, spouse, MRI device, or doctor; God knows your days and has a perfect plan for your life; God's perfect plan for your life includes and incorporates every relevant fact of your life today. Hey, when we realize this, we have one clear response to our challenges, and it is what God calls us to here:

¹⁰ Be still, and know that I am God.

(Psalm 46:10)

God is not just all knowing, He is also all generous and wants to share His wisdom with His children. He is looking for opportunities to share His wisdom; our job is simply to ask. Solomon, a person just like us, prayed for wisdom, and God gave Solomon great wisdom. He wants to do the same for you and me.

> [5] If any of you lacks wisdom, let him ask God, who gives generously to all without reproach, and it will be given him.
>
> *(James 1:5)*

Every problem we face God has already solved. That is right, the very thing you are anxious about, God has already solved the puzzle and put the pieces together on the board of your life. We don't have problems God cannot solve; we have problems we don't trust God to solve. The problem is not God's knowledge; the problem is we are too busy and too sophisticated to simply ask Him to help us.

We must grow out of our fear and our failure to fully lean on and trust our all-knowing God with all things, large and small. Don't be afraid to say, "Lord, show me where my keys are . . . what do I need to say to this person . . . help me with my math problem by giving me clarity of mind so I might use this wonderful instrument you have given me that we call a brain." "I just don't know what I should do!" "I don't know what the next step is; I just don't know what to do now." "There are so many things I have gotten wrong; I wish I knew how to live better, how to live life victoriously." There is no limit to the statements we could plug in here to demonstrate how each of us faces challenging moments when we do not know what the next best step is. This should not be—our all-knowing God is an all-loving Father and wants us to simply say, "Father, help me."

God knows all things, and He wants us to know everything we need to know. God loves you more than you love yourself. In Christ, God has adopted you into

His family; He is your Father. Whatever problem you face today, God is the answer, the very best answer for you. We are not waiting on God; He is waiting on you and me.

> ¹¹ If you then, who are evil, know how to give good gifts to your children, how much more will your Father who is in heaven give good things to those who ask him!
>
> *(Matthew 7:11)*

The question is not whether God is willing to give you good gifts, the question is not whether God is able to give you good gifts, and the question is not whether God knows what you need or not. The question is: Do we know God well enough to realize that He knows all things? He is waiting to hear and answer our questions and our prayers.

> ²⁶ Likewise the Spirit helps us in our weakness. For we do not know what to pray for as we ought, but the Spirit himself intercedes for us with groanings too deep for words. ²⁷ And he who searches hearts knows what is the mind of the Spirit, because the Spirit intercedes for the saints according to the will of God. ²⁸ And we know that for those who love God all things work together for good, for those who are called according to his purpose.
>
> *(Romans 8:26-28)*

> ¹⁴ I am the good shepherd. I know my own and my own know me, ¹⁵ just as the Father knows me and I know the Father; and I lay down my life for the sheep.
>
> *(John 10:14-15)*

²⁵ At that time Jesus declared, "I thank you, Father, Lord of heaven and earth, that you have hidden these things from the wise and understanding and revealed them to little children; ²⁶ yes, Father, for such was your gracious will. ²⁷ All things have been handed over to me by my Father, and no one knows the Son except the Father, and no one knows the Father except the Son and anyone to whom the Son chooses to reveal him. ²⁸ Come to me, all who labor and are heavy laden, and I will give you rest. ²⁹ Take my yoke upon you, and learn from me, for I am gentle and lowly in heart, and you will find rest for your souls. ³⁰ For my yoke is easy, and my burden is light."

(Matthew 11:25-30)

To know God, who knows all, is to know that all will be well today. I know of no greater peace and joy than to know God and know He is aware and able to handle whatever comes our way today. When we think of God and we reflect that He knows all things, we are strengthened and encouraged.

² I want them to be encouraged and knit together by strong ties of love. I want them to have complete confidence that they understand God's mysterious plan, which is Christ himself. ³ In him lie hidden all the treasures of wisdom and knowledge.

(Colossians 2:2-3, NLT)

³⁰ For all the nations of the world seek after these things, and your Father knows that you need them. ³¹ Instead, seek his kingdom, and these things will be added to you.

(Luke 12:30-31)

Prayer recognizing that God knows all things:

Father, we are so excited to have a Father who knows everything. Lord, there is nothing You do not know. You know the very hairs on each of our heads, You know the number of grains of sand on all the beaches of all the bodies of water throughout the world. You know where our car keys are, You know where our children are, You know the test results before the test is taken, You know all things, and You love us and care for us and have a plan for us that is wonderful. Father, we rest in Your knowledge. We confess there is so much we don't know, but what we do know is that You, O Lord, are the source of all knowledge, and we trust in You completely. Right now we ask You to help us rest in You, the all-knowing God who loves us and cares for us. We don't have to wonder what is around the next curve or over the next hill because the God who loves us knows all these things, and we rest in Your knowledge. God, we trust and rest in You.

Amen.

Chapter 12

God Is Omnipresent

WHERE ARE YOU, GOD? I need You, God! God, please answer. Come to me, God.

"He is here, hallelujah! He is here, amen! You will never be the same."[29]

When the storms of life are raging—finances, family, marriage, illness, job, children, grandchildren, neighbors, prison, addiction, depression, desperation—we want to know, "Where is God?" I need to know right this very moment, in this hour of tribulation, "Where is God?" When we learn that our life has just taken a tragic turn and we have no idea how to even draw our next breath, there is nothing more important to know than "Where is God right now?"

¹Fear not, for I have redeemed you;
I have called you by name, you are mine.

² When you pass through the waters, I will be with you;
and through the rivers, they shall not overwhelm you;

when you walk through fire you shall not be burned,
and the flame shall not consume you.

³*For I am the LORD your God,*
the Holy One of Israel, your Savior.

(Isaiah 43:1-3)

When I was a child, our phone system went through a local operator in downtown Meadville: Mrs. Guice. I think we had a number like twenty-five or something, but you didn't really use numbers; it was all names, and Mrs. Guice generally knew where everyone was at any given point in time. When I was about five or six years old, a telephone conversation in our little local phone system went something like this: I pick up the phone (no dial on it) and say these words: "Do you know where my mama is?" The voice, Mrs. Guice, would answer with something along these lines: "Your mother was at Faye's Beauty Shop, but I think she left there. She might be at Aldridge Meat Market because I know she and your daddy have company coming tonight." If I am exaggerating any, it's by precious little. We knew where our parents were (and presumably they kept up with us in the same fashion), and that was comforting. Yet it is infinitely more important and comforting to know where God is — to know that no matter how bad things are going, you can know right where He is and be able to absolutely count on His presence!

The most beautiful and empowering knowledge we can have is simply this: God is here; He is not going anywhere. God is not just here, but He is here with a plan for your life. A plan to bless you and care for you and prosper you. God is omnipresent, and He is bigger than whatever is going on in your life. God is never caught off guard, and no challenge ever overcomes His provision, His love, His peace, and His plan for you.

When hard times hit, it is so important to have friends and family close by. Yet, no matter how much comfort a family member or a friend might be to us, there is no presence like the presence of God. No matter how close we are to another person, no matter how much or how well we connect with them, there are things they cannot know, cannot do for us or with us, and there are needs they are not capable of addressing—they are not even made to address those needs. God alone is able. God knows you intimately! He loves and cares for you more than you love yourself. "God, I know You love me so much; I just wish You were here, God!" Well, hallelujah, He is here!

> [6] Be strong and courageous. Do not fear or be in dread of them, for it is the LORD your God who goes with you. He will not leave you or forsake you.
>
> *(Deuteronomy 31:6)*

God, who created everything, who is all loving, all powerful, and all knowing, is right here with you! Lord, have mercy, what a profoundly amazing and transforming truth. When we wrap our minds around the truth of God's presence and embrace His promises to be with us and never leave us, we will never be the same. We will no longer be overwhelmed by our fears, anxieties, and worries; the knowledge of the presence of God transforms us into bold, peaceful, strong, and effective children of the Most High God who is, hallelujah, right here with us.

In Christ, we are new creations. But most of us are not living out all that we are in Christ. We all struggle, to one degree or another, to fully embrace all we are and all we have in our relationship in Christ Jesus. No truth is more liberating and empowering than the truth of the very presence of the very God with you right now, right where you are! To know God's presence in this real, practical, personal manner is absolutely life changing—we should never be the same again. God is here! I never need to fear, feel lonely, feel left out, feel unloved again—God is here!

So, when the worst possible news comes—when the test results are cancer; when depression hits like a ton of bricks on our chest; when the one we thought we could count on the most says, "I want a divorce, I don't love you anymore"; even when someone comes to the door to deliver the most devastating news— God is present. He says, "I will not leave you; I will not forsake you; I will be with you always!" We may be so devastated we cannot raise our head, but we can raise our hearts because, hallelujah, the God who created the Milky Way, who parted the Red Sea, who put Mount Everest in place, who sent His Son Jesus to die in my place, in your place—He is here, He loves you, and He is not leaving. To know God is present is to live life in the way God intended, sweeter and more beautiful than we ever imagined.

Who do I say God is? God is here! God is with me! When you and I embrace this simple fact—God is omnipresent—it's a game changer, a life transformer, the source of true peace and strength in even the worst of life's storms. God tells us many times in Scripture that life comes with difficulties. The truth is, those difficulties are ultimately for our benefit. We know that, but we think, "Lord, I know You are helping me by using this (fill in the blank) circumstance to shape me into the person I need to be. But, Lord, I am so afraid and so alone. Please help me, God!" He has answered, and He has said,

[5] *"I will never fail you.*
I will never abandon you."

[6] *So we can say with confidence,*
"The LORD is my helper,
so I will have no fear.
What can mere people do to me?"
(Hebrews 13:5-6, NLT)

When we know that God is here, we know—no matter what—it is well with our soul. In fact, we are way better than okay; we are good, strong, determined, and focused. We are facing life with purpose and passion. We can rejoice in the midst of life's most difficult moments (hours, days, years) because the Lord is with us.

[5] Just as I was with Moses, so I will be with you. I will not leave you or forsake you.
(Joshua 1:5)

God is with you no matter what. When life hits you in the face (and it will), you can say, as was written by a man many years ago, "It is well with my soul." Many of us have read about the triumph-from-tragedy story of Horatio G. Spafford. He was a Chicago lawyer living in the mid-1800s. He lost most of his assets, his son, and his four daughters. Following those unbelievable tragedies, he was yet able to pen these words:

It Is Well with My Soul[30]

When peace, like a river, attendeth my way,
When sorrows like sea billows roll;
Whatever my lot, Thou hast taught me to say,
It is well, it is well with my soul.

REFRAIN

It is well, with my soul,
It is well, with my soul,
It is well, it is well, with my soul.

Though Satan should buffet, though trials should come,
Let this blest assurance control,
That Christ hath regarded my helpless estate,
And hath shed His own blood for my soul.

REFRAIN

My sin, oh the bliss of this glorious thought!
My sin, not in part but the whole,
Is nailed to His cross, and I bear it no more,
Praise the Lord, praise the Lord, O my soul!

REFRAIN

For me, be it Christ, be it Christ hence to live:
If Jordan above me shall roll,
No pang shall be mine, for in death as in life
Thou wilt whisper Thy peace to my soul.

REFRAIN

And Lord haste the day, when my faith shall be sight,
The clouds be rolled back as a scroll;
The trump shall resound, and the Lord shall descend,
Even so, it is well with my soul.

REFRAIN

⁶ Do not be anxious about anything, but in everything by prayer and supplication with thanksgiving let your requests be made known unto God. ⁷ And the peace of God, which surpasses all understanding, will guard your hearts and your minds in Christ Jesus.

(Philippians 4:6-7)

When we have the right picture of God, the picture of who God is and where God is, we can know He is not a God far away, He is not a God who looks at us from a distant place. Instead, He is a God who is right here with us! We can sit by the bed of our loved one, we can pass through the valley of the shadow of death, we can face the finances that don't get us to the end of the month, we can know that even though he or she is leaving, even though the child is far from where we want and would have them to be—in the midst of all these tragedies, we are not alone, we do not have to despair, for the Lord our God is with us. He will not leave us, and so it is well with our soul. Praise be to God forever and ever.

As God was to Moses, as God was to Joshua:

⁵ No man shall be able to stand before you all the days of your life. Just as I was with Moses, so I will be with you. I will not leave you or forsake you. ⁶ Be strong and courageous, for you shall cause this people to inherit the land that I swore to their fathers to give them. ⁷ Only be strong and very courageous, being careful to do according to all the law that Moses my servant commanded you. Do not turn from it to the right hand or to the left, that you may have good success wherever you go. ⁸ This Book of the Law shall not depart from your mouth, but

you shall meditate on it day and night, so that you may be careful to do according to all that is written in it. For then you will make your way prosperous, and then you will have good success. ⁹ Have I not commanded you? Be strong and courageous. Do not be frightened, and do not be dismayed, for the LORD your God is with you wherever you go.

(Joshua 1:5-9)

So is God with you and me and all who are in Christ. He is here, hallelujah; He is here, amen.

Prayer to acknowledge God's presence in our life:

Lord, today life is knocking us down. We don't know what to do. We don't have the answers. Lord, we don't even know the right questions. We have never been here, and we are afraid. Help us, Lord, to remember right now that You are not a God far away. You are God right here. You are with us, and it is well with our soul. You are with us, Lord, and even if the day gets worse, You are not leaving. You have promised never to leave us. Because You are here, Lord, we can get through this day. We thank you, Lord, for Your presence with us and Your promise to never leave us. Lord, help us to know that Your presence with us is not based on how we feel. I don't have to feel You; I just have to know You are God, You are here, and You are not going anywhere.

Amen.

Chapter 13

God Is Merciful

²² *The steadfast love of the LORD never ceases;*
his mercies never come to an end;

²³ *they are new every morning;*
great is your faithfulness.

²⁴ *"The LORD is my portion," says my soul,*
"therefore I will hope in him."
                              (Lamentations 3:22-24)

GOD IS A MERCIFUL GOD. When we wake up each morning, God's mercy for you and for me is fresh and new for this new day in which we now live. We need mercy for today, and that is exactly what our merciful God meets us with. As with each of God's attributes, God's mercy is just what we need, right when we need it.

We all have events and circumstances in our lives that we would rather no one ever find out about. There are thoughts, words, and actions that we wish had never occurred. We cannot imagine God loving us if He really knew all that we know about our own lives and our motives. When I am really honest about who I am, what I have done, and what I have failed to do, my initial reaction is fear of God's punishment and judgment falling on me at any moment. I know I do not deserve to live; I know I deserve God's harshest judgment for the sin in my life.

Then I remember mercy! Through God's mercy we are not consumed; His mercy is new every morning. We love mercy, don't we? Mercy is when we don't get what we deserve. A mother once came to the Emperor Napoleon to plead for mercy for her son who had been sentenced to die. Napoleon responded that her son did not deserve mercy. She said, "Sir, if he deserved it, it would not be mercy." Mercy is God not giving us the punishment we deserve for our sin against Him.

Returning to our hidden sin that we believe puts us just out of reach of forgiveness by a God who is holy and just, we think, "If God really knew who I am, there is no way He would ever forgive me; if God really knew me, His judgment would fall upon me with a vengeance. I have done things that God could never forgive." We read and hear over and over how God is a God of justice. How could a God of justice be merciful to me if He really knew me? Would God, could God really forgive me and not punish me for that sin I would never dare tell anyone, that sin so bad I don't even talk to myself about it? Is a just God able to show mercy to me for even my deepest sins?

One of the things we have to know about God is that God's justice is completely comfortable with God's mercy. God's mercy is completely at ease with God's holiness. This is who God is. God is not like us in our fickle way of being one way today and different tomorrow. We have moments when we feel forgiving and loving, but we also have moments when we feel like we are ready for some justice and "people are not going to enjoy that." Those are our feelings in the moment. God does not feel merciful; we are not speaking here of God's feelings—we are looking at *who God is*! God is merciful!

It must be said and clearly understood that God does not and cannot choose to just ignore our sin. God does not and cannot forgive our sin without payment. The payment for our sin, the foundation of God's mercy extended to us, is the life, death, burial, and resurrection of Jesus Christ. While we were still in our sin, Christ died for us (see Romans 5:8). So God's mercy is not a winking at sin; it is the one sacrifice that paid for all sin for all time.

God's mercy is based solely on the finished work of Jesus. How can we ever cease to praise Him who knew no sin but who became sin that we might become the righteousness of God in Christ Jesus? How can we not love and serve Him who died that we might receive mercy we could never deserve because Jesus willingly took on our punishment for our sin, which He did not and could not deserve—Him being without sin and perfect in every way?

> [3] Blessed be the God and Father of our Lord Jesus Christ! According to his great mercy, he has caused us to be born again to a living hope through the resurrection of Jesus Christ from the dead, [4] to an inheritance that is imperishable, undefiled, and unfading, kept in heaven for you, [5] who by God's power are being guarded through faith for a salvation ready to be revealed in the last time.
>
> *(1 Peter 1:3-5)*

An MRI of God (if there was such a thing) would reveal that, through and through, God is merciful (as well as loving, just, holy, eternal, infinite, all knowing, all powerful). Mercy is not something God does; it is who God is. Each and every one of God's attributes work together in perfect synchronization. He is not a just God on Mondays and a merciful God on Tuesdays. We do not have to think, "I'd better get this prayer done on God's mercy day." No! God is who He is, and He never changes (this is another attribute addressed in an upcoming chapter). God is completely just while being completely merciful and loving and gracious and fair and kind in all that He is and all that He does.

What does God's mercy mean for me? What is God's mercy, and how does it apply to my life? Isn't God tired of being merciful to me? He did that for me yesterday, but I don't think He is going to be inclined to be merciful to me again today, right? Wrong. We have to, as much as we can, come to understand God and His mercy as He interacts with our lives. His mercies are new every morning for me and for you.

God has told us we are not to continue in sin. In fact, He has warned us that no one who has been born again, who is truly in Christ, will keep on sinning as the regular course of their life. Yet He also recognizes that as we seek Him, by His grace, we will fall down daily. That is why He said,

> [4] Everyone who makes a practice of sinning also practices lawlessness; sin is lawlessness. [5] You know that he appeared in order to take away sins, and in him there is no sin. [6] No one who abides in him keeps on sinning; no one who keeps on sinning has either seen him or

known him. [7] Little children, let no one deceive you. Whoever practices righteousness is righteous, as he is righteous. [8] Whoever makes a practice of sinning is of the devil, for the devil has been sinning from the beginning. The reason the Son of God appeared was to destroy the works of the devil. [9] No one born of God makes a practice of sinning, for God's seed abides in him, and he cannot keep on sinning because he has been born of God. [10] By this it is evident who are the children of God, and who are the children of the devil: whoever does not practice righteousness is not of God, nor is the one who does not love his brother.

(1 John 3:4-10)

From Scripture, from experiences in life, from living and falling on my face, here is my appreciation of how God interacts with His children: To be in Christ is to be born again; it means old things have passed away and all things have become new—spiritually. But we still live inside the same old "house," and that "house," our flesh and its desires, will battle with us daily as long as we are wearing these human suits. In my life, there has never been a day, maybe not an hour, when I could say that there was not a word, a thought, or a deed that missed the mark (sin). So, my life, by the mercy and grace of God alone, is on a higher plane; I no longer sin as the regular course of my being, but I do sin regularly, daily in either my thoughts, words, or actions.

We are all hopeless apart from the finished work of Christ. In Christ, the course of our life is toward Him and away from the old way, and we say, by the grace of God, "I am not who I want to be, but I am ahead of where I used to be." The course of my life today is led by the Spirit, but every day, in one way or another, the flesh wins a temporary skirmish and I say, think, or do things I should not. So I am much in need of God's mercy—that is, for God not to give me what I deserve (eternal death right now) but instead to give me what I don't deserve (His grace), which is forgiveness that is fully accomplished by and in Christ. I have just told you what I think. If it deviates from the entire counsel of Scripture in any way, then it is not from God and you should absolutely reject what anyone says (including me) that departs from the whole truth of God found in His Holy Word, the Bible.

So, we need to know God has called us out of sin into righteousness. But the righteousness that allows us to come to God is not my righteous acts but the finished work of Christ. Here is one place we read this truth:

> ¹ My dear children, I am writing this to you so that you will not sin. But if anyone does sin, we have an advocate who pleads our case before the Father. He is Jesus Christ, the one who is truly righteous. ² He himself is the sacrifice that atones for our sins—and not only our sins but the sins of all the world.
>
> *(1 John 2:1-2, NLT)*

We have to acknowledge our complete dependence upon God every single moment of every single day. In First John we also read this:

> ⁵ This is the message we have heard from him and proclaim to you, that God is light, and in him is no darkness at all. ⁶ If we say we have fellowship with him while we walk in darkness, we lie and do not practice the truth. ⁷ But if we

walk in the light, as he is in the light, we have fellowship with one another, and the blood of Jesus his Son cleanses us from all sin. [8] If we say we have no sin, we deceive ourselves, and the truth is not in us. [9] If we confess our sins, he is faithful and just to forgive us our sins and to cleanse us from all unrighteousness. [10] If we say we have not sinned, we make him a liar, and his word is not in us.

(1 John 1:5-10)

Yes, you can count on God's mercy. His mercy is fresh and new this morning and every morning. Your sins and my sins have been fully paid for. That work was done by Christ, who proclaimed from the cross that He had finished His work of paying for our sins—Paid in Full![31]

God is a merciful God, and those mercies extend to all who are in Christ Jesus. There is no other way, but we need no other way because we have God's promise:

[8] For by grace you have been saved through faith. And this is not your own doing; it is the gift of God, [9] not a result of works, so that no one may boast.

(Ephesians 2:8-9)

Because God is merciful, we do not drag a past full of failures along behind us. Today, in Christ, we stand before God clothed with the righteousness of Christ. We are His children. The mercy of God is at work in our lives. It is so important for us to have sound and true thoughts when we think of who God is. We can know with assurance that God is a merciful God.

Prayer thanking God for His mercy:

Father, you are a merciful God. You do not give us what we deserve; instead, You show mercy to us every day. You promise us that Your mercy is never ending; it is new to us, in Christ Jesus, every morning. Father, we thank You that our standing with You is not measured by what we have done but by what Christ has done for us. Christ has graciously enabled us, as we fully trust in and rely on Him, to stand in the shower of Your mercy, which is without measure. Thank You, Father, for Your mercy in our lives today and every day.

Amen.

Chapter 14

God Is Just

GOD IS A JUST GOD in every way. He is just in how He treats us. He is just in how He treats sin. Just is a part of who God is every bit as much as His holiness, His power, and His mercy. God must be just; anything less and He would not in fact be God. God as a just God is Him always treating us justly; it is Him having Christ pay the price for justice by dying in our place; it is Him not turning a blind eye to sin but requiring it be paid for in full. God is a just God in every way.

Sometimes we might think, "Oh, God has been so loving; He is probably ready to bring His justice down on me by now." Each of God's attributes is completely consistent with all of His other attributes. God's justice does not have to give way to God's mercy or love. God's justice and God's love are not two opposing forces; they are one. God is completely just. God is completely loving. God's loving justice is infinite and unchanging.

What does "God is just" mean in your life today? It means we need to relax and let go of the idea that we have to find a way to get over God's bar of justice—we can't, we never could. Jesus did that for us.

> ⁶ For while we were still weak, at the right time Christ died for the ungodly. ⁷ For one will scarcely die for a righteous person—though perhaps for a good person one would dare even to die— ⁸ but God shows his love for us in that while we were still sinners, Christ died for us. ⁹ Since, therefore, we have now been justified by his blood, much more shall we be saved by him from the wrath of God. ¹⁰ For if while we were enemies we were reconciled to God by the death of his Son, much more, now that we are reconciled, shall we be saved by his life. ¹¹ More than that, we also rejoice in God through our Lord Jesus Christ, through whom we have now received reconciliation.
>
> *(Romans 5:6-11)*

We need to live our lives with an acute awareness that God hates sin and understand why! Sin cost Jesus! Sin is not something God can just sweep under the rug or wink at, saying "Oh, I love you; it'll be okay." It will not be okay; God hates sin. God is holy and can in no way ignore sin:

> ²³ For the wages of sin is death, but the free gift of God is eternal life in Christ Jesus our Lord.
> *(Romans 6:23)*

God created us for the express purpose of being in relationship with Him, honoring and glorifying Him in our lives. But we have all sinned, and God, as a completely holy God, can have nothing to do with sin. Because God is just, there has to be a way to deal with our sin, a way for us to be reconciled to God. God's justice and love are in perfect harmony—God cannot be loving without being just, and for God to be just, sin has to be paid for.

> [21] But now the righteousness of God has been manifested apart from the law, although the Law and the Prophets bear witness to it— [22] the righteousness of God through faith in Jesus Christ for all who believe. For there is no distinction: [23] for all have sinned and fall short of the glory of God, [24] and are justified by his grace as a gift, through the redemption that is in Christ Jesus, [25] whom God put forward as a propitiation by his blood, to be received by faith. This was to show God's righteousness, because in his divine forbearance he had passed over former sins. [26] It was to show his righteousness at the present time, so that he might be just and the justifier of the one who has faith in Jesus.
>
> *(Romans 3:21-26)*

As the hymn says, "Jesus paid it all, all to Him I owe; sin had left a crimson stain, He washed it white as snow."[32] God is holy and hates sin; He sent His Son to die for our sins. We need to know that God's justice is a really big deal.

Never make light of sin! Sin is not a big deal; sin is a huge deal. Sin is a huge deal because it is completely contrary to God. Sin is vile darkness, and God is justice and light; the two have nothing in common and are in fact direct opposites. God is opposed to sin in any size, shape, form, or fashion.

The world around us is screaming out the words of Bob Dylan's prophetic sixties hit "The Times They Are a Changin'." Some claim the world is changing, but a review of history reveals nothing has really changed.

Sin is no different today than thousands of years ago. Society will not and cannot exist long enough to change God's mind about sin. It is foolishness for us to say today, "Well, we live in a modern society, and it has changed the way we look at things." No doubt, it is true that society has changed its views on things. *But God has not changed!* God cannot change. God is just. God hates sin. God sent His only Son to die to pay for sin. God's justice is as much a part of who God is as His love is an essential part of God.

We have to look at God's justice this way: I am a sinner; God can have nothing to do with sin; I have to acknowledge my sin and trust in Christ because that is the only way my sin is covered—through Jesus' perfect full and final payment for my sin and yours. If I pretend to be somehow above sin or exempt from its effects, I am a liar and have no place at God's table.

> [9] If we confess our sins, he is faithful and just to forgive us our sins and to cleanse us from all unrighteousness. [10] If we say we have not sinned, we make him a liar, and his word is not in us.
> [1] My little children, I am writing these things to you so that you may not sin. But if anyone does sin, we have an advocate with the Father, Jesus Christ the righteous. [2] He is the propitiation for our sins, and not for ours only but also for the sins of the whole world.
>
> *(1 John 1:9-10, 2:1-2)*

"For God so loved the world" (John 3:16)—you and me—so we need to, in fact we must, embrace God's love but also His justice. We need to live with an awareness of how God sees sin and how He must deal with sin. God is a just God—all the time, for all time.

Prayer acknowledging God as a just God:

Father, you are a holy God and have nothing to do with sin. You sent Your Son to die for our sins. You have called us out of sin into the light of Your righteousness. Lord, may we never pretend that sin is okay; it is not okay. It is against You that we sin. May we all see sin for what it is—absolutely vile and offensive to God—then turn from it, repent of it, and walk in the light of Your Word. You are a just God, and we thank You for atoning for our sins through Jesus. May we live our lives with the full knowledge that Jesus paid it all; all to Him we owe. We acknowledge that sin debt, and we give eternal thanks to You, Lord, for Your mercy today and always.

Amen.

Chapter 15

God Is Gracious

Amazing grace! how sweet the sound,
That saved a wretch like me!
I once was lost, but now am found,
Was blind, but now I see.

'Twas grace that taught my heart to fear,
And grace my fears relieved;
How precious did that grace appear
The hour I first believed!

Thro' many dangers, toils and snares,
I have already come;
'Tis grace hath bro't me safe thus far,
And grace will lead me home.

The Lord has promised good to me,
His Word my hope secures;
He will my shield and portion be
As long as life endures.

When we've been there ten thousand years,
Bright shining as the sun,
We've no less days to sing God's praise
Than when we first begun.[33]

This most famous of hymns was written in 1772, probably as a prayer, by a born-again slave trader named John Newton. It is solid theology and experientially tells the story of all who are in Christ—who have been born again. I identify with each and every word. It tells us of grace, the amazing grace of God that is a part of who our heavenly Father is.

Grace is absolutely key to our daily lives in many ways. Nowhere does God's grace appear more prominently and providentially than here:

> [8] For by grace you have been saved through faith. And this is not your own doing; it is the gift of God.
>
> *(Ephesians 2:8)*

Grace is the most precious substance of which I know. Grace is the precious gift of God reaching down the hand of a King to a hopeless beggar like me, who is utterly hopeless apart from the saving grace of God.

God is a gracious God, and if this is all we ever knew of God, it is sufficient to fuel an unending hymn of praise from all who taste of Him who is grace without measure—Father, Son, and Holy Spirit.

God is a God of grace! His grace amazes anyone and everyone who is living in it. Yes, we live in grace—God's unmerited favor[34]—bestowed upon us bountifully day by day. When we awakened this morning, that was God's grace. When we draw in a breath of air, that is God's grace. When we lie down and when we get up, when we move and when we are still, when we breathe and when we cease to breathe—each and all of these represent God's grace.

[16] For from his fullness we have all received, grace upon grace.

(John 1:16)

Look at that same verse from the Amplified Bible[35]:

[16] For out of His fullness [the superabundance of His grace and truth] we have all received grace upon grace [spiritual blessing upon spiritual blessing, favor upon favor, and gift heaped upon gift].

(John 1:16, AMP)

Each one of God's attributes is the very essence of God, and they are all needed for our daily lives. While I know we need each one of God's attributes, I say, without hesitation, that God's grace ministers to me personally in a deep and profound way that seems to equal all of the other attributes combined. God's grace is present in every aspect of our lives; we are standing in God's grace, and we are awash in waves of grace. Thanks be to God, who is gracious without measure.

How does God's grace change how we look at and maneuver through a typical day? When we are blind to God's grace, it is just an undercover angel of sorts who is at work in our lives, and we are blissfully ignorant of it. But when we wake up to God's presence and the fullness of who God is, His grace comes to us out of everything the day brings. I am writing this paragraph sitting outside on an early spring morning in Ocean Springs, Mississippi, and the clover and the leaves are swaying in the breeze, doves are cooing, other birds are singing, and the sun's dappled rays are passing through the live oaks as the squirrels run to and fro. God's grace is blessing my skin, eyes, and ears.

Grace is sweet to the ear and a blessing to the soul. How does grace impact your daily life? Well, you cannot taste grace, you cannot see or hold grace, yet grace is sweeter to the taste than the richest of chocolate; grace feels better than the finest linen on your body; you may not hold grace, but grace holds you and me through the worst of times. How sweet is the sound of God's grace in our lives?

God's grace sounds mighty sweet in our salvation:

> [8] For by grace you have been saved through faith. And this is not your own doing; it is the gift of God, [9] not a result of works, so that no one may boast.
>
> *(Ephesians 2:8-9)*

God's grace is sweet when we know we have been redeemed by grace:

> [22] For there is no distinction: [23] for all have sinned and fall short of the glory of God, [24] and are justified by his grace as a gift, through the redemption that is in Christ Jesus, [25] whom God put forward as a propitiation by his blood, to be received by faith. This was to show God's righteousness, because in his divine forbearance he had passed over former sins.
>
> *(Romans 3:22-25)*

God's grace is how we stand, how we keep from falling, and how we have and occupy the place we enjoy in life. It is not just about standing but about everything we experience in our present life including breath, heartbeat, thoughts, words . . .

[1] Therefore, since we have been justified by faith, we have peace with God through our Lord Jesus Christ. [2] Through him we have also obtained access by faith into this grace in which we stand, and we rejoice in hope of the glory of God.

(Romans 5:1-2)

God's grace sounds especially sweet in the face of my daily failures, which are more appropriately called sin:

[20] Now the law came in to increase the trespass, but where sin increased, grace abounded all the more, [21] so that, as sin reigned in death, grace also might reign through righteousness leading to eternal life through Jesus Christ our Lord.

(Romans 5:20-21)

When you face the challenges of life today, remember it is also God's grace that allows this challenge to come; it is God's grace that empowers you to work through the challenge; and it is God's grace that keeps the challenge from being more than you can handle.

[7] So to keep me from becoming conceited because of the surpassing greatness of the revelations, a thorn was given me in the flesh, a messenger of Satan to harass me, to keep me from becoming conceited. [8] Three times I pleaded with the Lord about this, that it should leave me. [9] But he said to me, "My grace is sufficient for you, for my power is made perfect in weakness." Therefore I will boast all the more gladly of my weaknesses, so that the power of Christ may rest upon me.

(2 Corinthians 12:7-9)

Here is verse 9 in the Amplified:

> [9] But He said to me, "My grace is sufficient for you [My lovingkindness and My mercy are more than enough—always available—regardless of the situation]; for [My] power is being perfected [and is completed and shows itself most effectively] in [your] weakness." Therefore, I will all the more gladly boast in my weaknesses, so that the power of Christ [may completely enfold me and] may dwell in me.
>
> *(2 Corinthians 12:9, AMP)*

Tragically we often find ourselves resisting God's grace. We resist God's grace when we try to demonstrate we can do life on our own. We just naturally want to take charge of and receive recognition for our transformation, so we resist grace. We want to be strong. We want to be heroes. Grace says, "You cannot even draw breath without God acting in and through His grace." God is saying, "Whatever you are facing, you cannot get through it, you just can't do it without Me." But He then goes on to assure us, "My grace is sufficient." He is saying, "You can't, but I can—and so you can in Me and through Me, by grace."

Every hour of every day we stand in complete dependence upon the grace of God. We are as dependent upon God's grace as a child in the womb is dependent in every way upon the mother. God's grace is giving us light and breath and sustenance for our bodies, souls, and spirits. Grace is God's daily manna given into our lives from above. We have never seen such a substance before, but it is the sweetest thing we will ever know and upon grace we depend.

The hymn "Amazing Grace" does in itself teach us profound lessons about God's grace. I am not speaking of the words or the story but the circumstances that gave rise to its being written. How many men, women, and children suffered and died at the hands of John Newton and his employers before God's grace brought Newton to salvation and the penning of this wonderful hymn."[36] God's grace is at work through very difficult circumstances to lead us to a place of awakening to God's goodness and our deep sin. Grace is good no matter what form it takes because God is its source and its dispenser, and the purpose and end of grace is our reconciliation with God. I have no explanation for this except to say as God has said:

> [8] *For my thoughts are not your thoughts,*
> *neither are your ways my ways, declares the* LORD.
>
> [9] *For as the heavens are higher than the earth,*
> *so are my ways higher than your ways*
> *and my thoughts than your thoughts.*
>
> *(Isaiah 55:8-9)*

God's grace in my life has been abundant. One act of God's grace in my life came through a comment by a fellow Christian about my character. I was wounded, deeply offended, and just incensed at the lack of real perception by this sister in Christ. The truth is, she was far too gentle and should have hit me twice as hard.[37] She commented on my pride, and God knew I respected her and that He could, by that act of grace, bring me to see a deep sin in my life—pride. Pride, by my understanding and experience, is the single most destructive sin. Pride is a complete anti-God state of mind. Pride says, "I am good, and God is lucky to have me on His team." I wish I could claim that one act of God's grace relieved me of pride, but it did not. However, God did use that comment to awaken me to the reality and depth of pride in my life. Since then God has continued to try to show me the depth of this sin in my life. Day by day He is chipping away at me, and each blow of His sculptor's tool is an act of God's grace. I thank God for His grace.

Grace often hits us with blows much more devastating than a little touch to our ego. There are times in everyone's life when life circumstances hit us so hard we do not believe we can even draw another breath. This is hard, but even in the midst of life's most devastating events, the grace of God is at work. Grace is a part of God, God loves you, God is in control—so grace is a part of every challenge we face in life. The grace part of life's challenges is often visible only when viewed in our rearview mirror after the storm has passed.

Here is what we can know, and this is a perfect example of why it is so important to know who God is: When God allows a devastating event to take place and we want to cry out, "Why, God? Why me, God? Why now, God?" it is crucial to know who God is.

> God is holy.
> God is all loving.
> God is all powerful.
> God is present.
> God is merciful.
> God is just.
> God is gracious in all things.

Here's a warning against us trying to make God look better: It is deeply troubling and often just adds more hurt when people come running into the middle of a tragedy and try to tell the hurting person why the tragedy occurred. That is wrong. We don't know why certain events happen. We are not in the place of God.

But there are some things we can know, and they are good to share at the right time (only the Holy Spirit can guide us to the right time): "This tragedy does not change God's loving presence, His gracious provision, or His perfect plan for your life. God's grace is sufficient. These things we know, and we cling to these truths in the storm." We can gently point others to the ultimate grace of God in the person of Christ, whom they can anchor to in the storm.

I can look back on many disasters and see God's grace at work: in bringing me and others through the calamity; in strengthening us for what would follow; in showing Himself strong in the midst of our weakest moment; in calling us to seek Him more than ever; and in bringing people into the kingdom, people into prayer, and people to a place where they had to make decisions that would impact people and families for generations to come. I rarely have the sense of what God is doing at the moment, but I know—and we can all know—God is at work and that we can trust Him in the midst of life's most devastating storms. He is a good, good Father, and He is perfect in all of His ways. God is a gracious God at all times, in all things, for all things, for you and for me.

Prayer acknowledging God's grace:

Father, thank You for the grace in which we now stand. Lord, help us to know that Your grace is the key to our salvation, but it is also the key to our very next breath, to our being able to love You, to love our neighbor, to think right thoughts, to speak right words, to take right actions and avoid wrong ones. Lord, Your grace amazes each of us. We thank You, Lord, for being gracious to us without limit. We confess right here and now, it is only by Your grace that we can even pray this feeble prayer. Lord, graciously lead us into a deeper awareness of the beauty and fullness of Your grace and our full dependence upon Your grace. May we come to the point in our lives, even now, that one drop of Your grace fully received by us is more exquisite than anything this earth has to offer. Thank You, Lord, for grace. In Jesus' name we pray.

Amen.

Chapter 16

God Is Sovereign

GOD IS OVER ALL; GOD can and will do all that He wills to do. There is no one and no thing over God. God is in control. God's sovereignty should be the most reassuring of God's many attributes. When the world and life in general make no sense, we can find deep comfort and peace in the fact that God, who is love and light and mercy and grace and perfect in all His ways, is also sovereign—absolutely in control. When we know God is in charge, we know peace. God—not the president, not congress, not a political party, not any one or more terrorist groups—is in charge. Nothing happens in this world that is beyond God's ultimate control.

We should not be angry or put off when non-Christians say things like, "If God allowed (fill in the blank) to happen, I want nothing to do with God." The things of God do not make sense to the mind of one who is dead in trespasses and sin (as every one of us were before God's grace reached us). On the other hand, the Body of Christ has to embrace God's sovereignty. I do not claim we will always understand why things happen; we will not. There are events recounted in the Bible I do not understand or enjoy reading about, and there are things happening every day I do not understand. Yet, I can say, "The God who created the heavens and the earth, who sent His Son to die for me, is sovereign, and I don't have to always understand Him to love, trust, and obey Him."

If I understood everything God caused or allowed, He would not be God. The truth is, I trust Him even more for the very reason that He is God and His ways are above my ways. The reality of life's difficult events is why (a) it is of ultimate importance that a person be born again spiritually so that spiritual things can be understood and enjoyed; and (b) we have to know God fully so we can trust Him completely in all things and at all times, especially in the midst of the storm.

Parents do things for their children that, to the child, seem anything but loving. The child does not have the same vision the parent has; the child can only see their immediate circumstances, and they do not understand the full implication of certain choices and actions by the parents. The parents are acting with a much deeper knowledge of what is needed. On a much higher level of both love and knowledge, God permits the free will of others to act for our good in ways that we do not understand. Our honest thoughts are "God has abandoned us. God does not love us. God is not a good God." Yet, like children, we cannot see what God sees.

> [28] And we know that for those who love God all things work together for good, for those who are called according to his purpose.
>
> *(Romans 8:28)*

We should never attempt to explain away God's actions and inactions in difficult circumstances. We are not in the place of God. We do not have His perspective. We do not know all that is going on; in fact, we know very little. In my opinion, and this is just my opinion, in the vast majority of tragedies, our responsibility is to love and quietly support those in pain. It is not our job to tell them what God is doing or why something is happening. What we can—and I believe should—do is simply stand on God's love and His presence and say to others, "I don't understand this tragedy, but what we do know is God loves you and He has promised never to leave you. Rest in Him and look to Him. He is the answer."

What I think does not matter, but what does matter is this: God is sovereign—He is in control. God is love. God is light. God is gracious. God is almighty. God is holy. God is all knowing. We do not have to understand the things God allows to happen, but we can know at the deepest level of our soul that whatever happens has happened under the loving watch of the one and only true and sovereign God. We can always trust Him and know that He knows more than us; He has a plan, and His plan, whether we can see it or not, is a perfect plan.

Some will say, "I don't trust God, and I don't even believe in God." We have to know one of two things: (1) God is God, and I can trust Him; or (2) there is no God and it is all just chance, and it doesn't matter because we are here for a few moments and then we go away forever. You do not have to accept my thoughts, but I can say with absolute assurance: I know that I know that I know that God is who He says and does what He promises. I know this because He has said this, and God always, always, always does what He says. I also know God's sovereignty because I have lived this—thanks be to God.

Here is what God has said through David about God's involvement in your life and my life:

> *13 For you formed my inward parts;*
> *you knitted me together in my mother's womb.*

> *14 I praise you, for I am fearfully and wonderfully made.*
> *Wonderful are your works;*
> *my soul knows it very well.*

> *15 My frame was not hidden from you,*
> *when I was being made in secret,*
> *intricately woven in the depths of the earth.*

> *16 Your eyes saw my unformed substance;*
> *in your book were written, every one of them,*
> *the days that were formed for me,*
> *when as yet there was none of them.*
>
> *(Psalm 139:13-16)*

God formed us and made us just as He wants us to be. We were perfectly placed in time, place, personality, and life circumstances to be used by God for His purposes. Our goal is to bring glory and honor to God as we are transformed into the likeness of Christ Jesus. Our life circumstances are a part of God's sovereignty and His plan, and life's events are moving toward that end.

Some would say that such thoughts about God's sovereignty and His placement of each of us are either blind faith or gross ignorance. I am not upset about those who put me down for my beliefs as a Christian. I have a personal love relationship with the Creator of this universe. He loves me so much that His Son died in my place and now represents me before God the Father in heaven, pleading my case. I have personally experienced and daily continue to personally experience wonderful love and contact with the Creator; by His grace I daily feel His very real presence and counsel in every area of my life. God's sovereignty does not work against my faith; it strengthens and grows my faith. That same God who gives me faith and grows my faith is also the one who allows me to love the very person who would speak down to me for my faith.

I am comfortable with my faith. I do not know the comfort level of those who criticize the faith of Christians but would gently say, "It seems to me the more difficult faith challenge is to believe that at some point in time a billion or so years ago nothing created something that is now the human body with all its intricacies; that the universe that works in perfect order just happened from that nothing; that a red rose came from that nothing; that an Alaskan salmon came from that same nothing and shall return to that nothing." I am not offended that the person who believes that also believes I am either stupid or clueless. I absolutely love and pray for that person, and I want him and her to have what I have—that they will soon join me in praising the God who is sovereign over them, over me, over all of us!

God is sovereign over all persons. God has the ability to use His sovereignty to the point of directing the specific actions of any person He wishes. We can read in Exodus how God caused Pharaoh to refuse to release the Jewish people. There are similar examples all throughout Scripture. I personally experienced God exercising His sovereignty to accomplish His will in a certain circumstance. There was a time when I went to a certain jail to ask permission to minister there. I was told in advance the officer over the jail prohibited personal contact with the prisoners; there was always a wall separating the two. I wanted to be able to shake hands and give pats on the shoulder, to stand side by side and look at the Bible together with the inmates. I prayed before I went, asking God to open that door and break down that wall. I did not mention the issue to the officer; I just trusted God to work out His will. If God wanted to break down the wall between the inmates and me, He would do that in His way and in His time.

I pulled up to the jail on my motorcycle and placed it all in God's hands. I felt like this whole effort rested on being able to get the wall of separation taken down, but I knew it was totally up to God. When I went into the jail, the officer over this large jail took the time to personally show me around. When we got to the location where the residents were brought to hear the sermon, the officer said, "The inmates will be here, and you will be" —he looked at me— "in there with them." Without me ever saying a word to anyone, God sovereignly worked out His purposes. God accomplished ministry there in that jail because He is sovereign. The Bible is filled with examples of God's sovereignty.

How is God's sovereignty important to our daily life? Knowing God is sovereign is the key to living joyful, peaceful lives in this world filled with challenges and threats. Please reflect on this: When we get the real picture of God's sovereignty over all things; when we bring that together with the knowledge that God loves us so much He sent His only Son to die in our place; when we know God has great plans for our lives and that God is almighty—then all fear fades away. This is a picture of God's perfect love, which casts out fear:

¹⁸ There is no fear in love, but perfect love casts out fear. For fear as to do with punishment, and whoever fears has not been perfected in love.

(1 John 4:18)

Knowing God is a sovereign God, we can face the day, the night, the diagnosis, the loss, whatever life throws our way, with absolute calm and trust and a sure knowledge that all is well—it is well with our soul. We need not fear any terrorist group, not their bombs, not their swords, not their jihad or any other thing they bring to the table. Why? Because I know my God is in control, and if they bring something bad against me, He will work it out for good. Let's look at a couple of examples from Scripture:

¹⁵ When Joseph's brothers saw that their father was dead, they said, "It may be that Joseph will hate us and pay us back for all the evil that we did to him." ¹⁶ So they sent a message to Joseph, saying, "Your father gave this command before he died: ¹⁷ 'Say to Joseph, "Please forgive the transgression of your brothers and their sin, because they did evil to you."' And now, please forgive the transgression of the servants of the God of your father." Joseph wept when they spoke to him. ¹⁸ His brothers also came and fell down before him and said, "Behold, we are your servants." ¹⁹ But Joseph said to them, "Do not fear, for am I in the place of God? ²⁰ As for you, you meant evil against me, but God meant it for good, to bring it about that many people should be kept alive, as they are today. ²¹ So do not fear; I will provide for you and your little ones." Thus he comforted them and spoke kindly to them.

(Genesis 50:15-21)

King Nebuchadnezzar declared that at the sound of certain music all people had to bow down and worship him. Shadrach, Meshach, and Abednego refused. They would only worship God. Why would anything bad happen to men who were doing good things?

[16]Shadrach, Meshach, and Abednego answered and said to the king, "O Nebuchadnezzar, we have no need to answer you in this matter. [17]If this be so, our God whom we serve is able to deliver us from the burning fiery furnace, and he will deliver us out of your hand, O king. [18]But if not, be it known to you, O king, that we will not serve your gods or worship the golden image that you have set up."

[19]Then Nebuchadnezzar was filled with fury, and the expression of his face was changed against Shadrach, Meshach, and Abednego. He ordered the furnace heated seven times more than it was usually heated. [20]And he ordered some of the mighty men of his army to bind Shadrach, Meshach, and Abednego, and to cast them into the burning fiery furnace. [21]Then these men were bound in their cloaks, their tunics, their hats, and their other garments, and they were thrown into the burning fiery furnace. [22]Because the king's order was urgent and the furnace overheated, the flame of the fire killed those men who took up Shadrach, Meshach, and Abednego. [23]And these three men, Shadrach, Meshach, and Abednego, fell bound into the burning fiery furnace.

[24]Then King Nebuchadnezzar was astonished and rose up in haste. He declared to his counselors, "Did we not cast three men bound into the fire?" They answered and said to the

king, "True, O king." ²⁵ He answered and said, "But I see four men unbound, walking in the midst of the fire, and they are not hurt; and the appearance of the fourth is like a son of the gods."

²⁶ Then Nebuchadnezzar came near to the door of the burning fiery furnace; he declared, "Shadrach, Meshach, and Abednego, servants of the Most High God, come out, and come here!" Then Shadrach, Meshach, and Abednego came out from the fire.

(Daniel 3:16-26)

Jesus lived a perfect life. God said, "This is my beloved Son, with whom I am well pleased" (Matthew 3:17). Yet Jesus was crucified, died, and was buried. How could a loving God allow this to happen to His own Son? First, I sure thank Him that He did; that God ordained those events is the only reason we are here now. Second, God does not look at things the way we look at things. God has perfect vision that is not bound by time or space. His will is consistent with His perfect love, mercy, grace, goodness, knowledge, and power. Whatever God does is just fine. I do not always understand. I do not always like God's will. But I can always, always, always trust God's sovereign will. Whatever God does or allows will work out for good for all those who are born-again believers trusting in Jesus Christ and called according to His purposes.

¹⁴ Then if my people who are called by my name will humble themselves and pray and seek my face and turn from their wicked ways, I will hear from heaven and will forgive their sins and restore their land.

(2 Chronicles 7:14, NLT)

It is vital to our daily lives and our growth in faith to know God. Knowing God in His absolute sovereignty is critical to our daily life. Let's close by quoting A. W. Tozer on the sovereignty of God:

God's sovereignty means that if there's anybody in this wide world of sinful men that should be restful and peaceful in an hour like this, it should be Christians. We should not be under the burden of apprehension and worry because we are the children of a God who is always free to do as He pleases. There is not one rope or chain or hindrance upon Him, because He is absolutely sovereign.

God is free to carry out His eternal purposes to their conclusions. I have believed this since I first became a Christian. I had good teachers who taught me this and I have believed it with increasing joy ever since. God does not play by ear, or doodle, or follow whatever happens to come into His mind or let one idea suggest another. God works according to the plans which He purposed in Christ Jesus before Adam walked in the garden, before the sun, moon and stars were made. God, who has lived all our tomorrows and carries time in His bosom, is carrying out His eternal purposes.

His eternal purposes will not change, however the prophetic teachers may change their minds or whatever contemporary theologians may decide is the right thing to believe. God Almighty has already given us His theology, and I don't give a snap of my finger for contemporary theology. I believe in theology, which is contemporary surely, but it is also as ancient as the throne of God and as eternal as the eternities to come. And we Christians are in this mighty river, being carried along by the sovereign purposes of God.

The sovereignty of God involves all authority and all power. I think you can see instantly that God could never be sovereign without the power to bring about His will or the authority to exercise His power. Kings, presidents and others who rule over men must have the authority to govern and the power to make good on that authority. A ruler cannot stand up and say, "Do this, please, if you feel like doing it." He says, "Do it," and then has an army and a police force behind him. He has authority to command and power to carry out his commands. And God has to have both of these.[38]

God is absolutely sovereign. I am so glad He is. Can you imagine what it would be like if you or I had any control over what happens in this world? God is sovereign; praise be to Him.

Prayer thanking God and acknowledging His sovereignty:

O sovereign God, You alone are Lord. You have set the earth and all of the universe in place. You created things exactly according to Your own plan. We were not there; we had no part in Your creation. You put each of us in the place You precisely and perfectly planned for us; we are all wonderfully and perfectly made according to Your sovereign will from before eternity. We can enter into this day and each day saying, "Lord, thank You that You, not us, are in charge of our life, this universe, and all that happens here. We don't understand all things, but in all things we trust You and know Your love, Your holiness, Your mercy, and Your sovereignty are fully at work, and we can rest and trust in You." Father, help us to embrace the full assurance we have when we know our loving Father is fully in control—no matter what. Lord, when we hurt and we don't know why, help us to know that if we, as sinful earthly parents, know how to give good gifts to our children, how much more do You give wonderful and perfect gifts to us. We admit we don't understand some of the things that come our way, but in the midst of trial and even tragedy we can say as Job did, "The LORD gave, and the LORD has taken away; blessed be the name of the LORD" (Job 1:21).

Amen.

Chapter 17

God Is Unchanging

WE LIVE IN A WORLD of change, a world where people are concerned by what is "trending," what is popular now. What do the latest polls show? What is in fashion now? What is the politically correct way of saying . . . ? We live in a world of change.

God does not change. God is not interested in what Wall Street, Main Street, or Back Street thinks is in vogue. God is the same always.

> [8] Jesus Christ is the same yesterday and today and forever.
>
> *(Hebrews 13:8)*

God doesn't change with the tide; in fact, He controls the tides, and yet He never changes. His mind is made up: He loves you, and He has a plan that will prosper you. He has set boundaries in this world that are here not to tickle our fancy but to save us from our own foolishness. There are only two ways to live in this world. We can be smart, make good choices, and live the life God called us to by honoring and revering Him, His Word, and His way:

> [7] The fear of the LORD is the beginning of knowledge;
> fools despise wisdom and instruction.
>
> (Proverbs 1:7)

Or we can follow the way of the world, being blown and tossed here and there by every wind of change and by whatever the current political correctness happens to be—in essence, despising the true wisdom and solid instruction that are ours in God's Word. God has laid out a plan, but it is not according to worldly ways; it is a plan based on God's perfect knowledge. He knows us, our weaknesses and our failures; God cares for us better than we could ever care for ourselves.

> [16] Don't be deceived, my dear brothers and sisters. [17] Every good and perfect gift is from above, coming down from the Father of the heavenly lights, who does not change like shifting shadows.
>
> (James 1:16-17, NIV)

I was born, raised, and lived most of my life in the small but beautiful corner of the world called Franklin County, Mississippi. For many years when you traveled U.S. Highway 98 through our county, you could count on seeing Mr. Cicero Nettles, at eighty-plus years of age, in his faded blue overalls, sitting in front of his house and waving at anyone who passed by. Stopping to visit Mr. Cicero was one of the greatest earthly blessings I ever experienced. He was a gentle, Christ-centered man with cornflower blue eyes shining brightly, a warm smile, and a firm embrace. A short time before his death, I visited him and was blessed to see that, even facing death, he was the same. He never changed; he was always Mr. Cicero, a strong, quiet, steady man who trusted in the God who never changes. He knew without a doubt that come what may, He could count on God in all weather. Mr. Cicero was one of those blessed earthly examples of God's unchanging character.

> ⁶ And I am certain that God, who began the good work within you, will continue his work until it is finally finished on the day when Christ Jesus returns.
>
> *(Philippians 1:6, NLT)*

We live in a topsy-turvy world where everything seems to be constantly changing. Today, more than ever, we need to know God, to know we can count on Him. We need to know that when everything around us is falling apart, when everything we thought of as dependable, when all that we once held dear is turned upside down, we can absolutely count on God. God is a firm foundation, and He never changes.

The world around us is telling us to forget about what the Bible says; this is a new day, and we need new ways. These are not new days and the ways of the world are not new; the world today is no different than at any other time in history. God is not intimidated or moved by the actions of the world. He has seen our failures since He put us here; He has revealed Himself to us and made known His truth. It is up to us to turn away from the changing world to the One who never changes, God, our shelter and resting place through all times.

Read these words from Paul's letter to the Romans that describe the world today just as perfectly as it did two thousand years ago:

¹⁹ They know the truth about God because he has made it obvious to them. ²⁰ For ever since the world was created, people have seen the earth and sky. Through everything God made, they can clearly see his invisible qualities—his eternal power and divine nature. So they have no excuse for not knowing God.

²¹ Yes, they knew God, but they wouldn't worship him as God or even give him thanks. And they began to think up foolish ideas of what God was like. As a result, their minds became dark and confused. ²² Claiming to be wise, they instead became utter fools. ²³ And instead of worshiping the glorious, ever-living God, they worshiped idols made to look like mere people and birds and animals and reptiles.

²⁴ So God abandoned them to do whatever shameful things their hearts desired. As a result, they did vile and degrading things with each other's bodies. ²⁵ They traded the truth about God for a lie. So they worshiped and served the things God created instead of the Creator himself, who is worthy of eternal praise! Amen. ²⁶ That is why God abandoned them to their shameful desires. Even the women turned against the natural way to have sex and instead indulged in sex with each other. ²⁷ And the men, instead of having normal sexual relations with women, burned with lust for each other. Men did shameful things with other men, and as a result of this sin, they suffered within themselves the penalty they deserved.

²⁸ Since they thought it foolish to acknowledge God, he abandoned them to their foolish thinking and let them do things that should never be done. ²⁹ Their lives became full of every kind

of wickedness, sin, greed, hate, envy, murder, quarreling, deception, malicious behavior, and gossip. [30] They are backstabbers, haters of God, insolent, proud, and boastful. They invent new ways of sinning, and they disobey their parents. [31] They refuse to understand, break their promises, are heartless, and have no mercy. [32] They know God's justice requires that those who do these things deserve to die, yet they do them anyway. Worse yet, they encourage others to do them, too.

(Romans 1:19-32, NLT)

Nothing has changed. We see people who reject God today acting just like the people who rejected God thousands of years ago. I want to make sure I am clear on this: None of us is any better—we have all sinned and fallen short (see Romans 3:23), and it is only by the saving work of Christ that any one of us is born again and thus saved from sin. The only way we overcome our old nature is by trusting in the finished work of Christ.

[4] But you belong to God, my dear children. You have already won a victory over those people, because the Spirit who lives in you is greater than the spirit who lives in the world. [5] Those people belong to this world, so they speak from the world's viewpoint, and the world listens to them. [6] But we belong to God, and those who know God listen to us. If they do not belong to God, they do not listen to us. That is how we know if someone has the Spirit of truth or the spirit of deception.

(1 John 4:4-6, NLT)

God is the same always. When life changes, we don't have to panic. We can know that an all-loving, holy, just, merciful God has not changed overnight. When everything around us is falling apart and it looks like life as we have known it is disappearing, we can rest in the absolute truth that God is unchanging. He loves you, He is sovereign, and He knows the circumstances; none of this has caught Him off guard. God is not going anywhere; He has promised to be with you, and He is. God never changes.

> ⁶ I am the LORD, and I do not change.
> *(Malachi 3:6, NLT)*

God does not change, and neither does His Word. There is no provision in the Word of God for changing times. God's Word says,

> ¹⁸ For truly, I say to you, until heaven and earth pass away, not an iota, not a dot, will pass from the Law until all is accomplished. ¹⁹ Therefore whoever relaxes one of the least of these commandments and teaches others to do the same will be called least in the kingdom of heaven, but whoever does them and teaches them will be called great in the kingdom of heaven.
> *(Matthew 5:18-19)*

This is what we have to know to live in this world in perfect peace: The God who created this world, who created you and me, is here; He is not going anywhere, and He does not change ever. The events of this day will not change who God is; no matter how horrific an event may be, God's love and presence and peace and power are still here. His love and His plan for your life are still the same—to bless you and prosper you in Christ Jesus. God is perfect in all of His ways.

Prayer thanking God that He is unchanging:

Gracious heavenly Father, thank You that we can count on You no matter what. You do not change; You are light, love, gracious, merciful, just, holy, ever present, all powerful, and all knowing, and neither You nor anything about You has ever changed—nor will You ever change. When we awake in the morning, we don't have to look outside or run to the television, the computer, or our cell phones to see what is going on in the world because You are and You always will be. No matter the weather, no matter the news, no matter the politics, no matter the diagnosis, no matter what anyone else says or does, You are God and You love us, You have a plan for us, You are coming back for us, and in Christ Jesus it is well with our soul. We thank You and praise You forever and ever.

Amen.

Chapter 18

God Is Holy

¹ Now Moses was keeping the flock of his fa-
ther-in-law, Jethro, the priest of Midian, and
he led his flock to the west side of the wilder-
ness and came to Horeb, the mountain of God.
² And the angel of the LORD appeared to him
in a flame of fire out of the midst of a bush. He
looked, and behold, the bush was burning, yet
it was not consumed. ³ And Moses said, "I will
turn aside to see this great sight, why the bush
is not burned." ⁴ When the LORD saw that he
turned aside to see, God called to him out of
the bush, "Moses, Moses!" And he said, "Here
I am." ⁵ Then he said, "Do not come near; take
your sandals off your feet, for the place on
which you are standing is holy ground." ⁶ And
he said, "I am the God of your father, the God
of Abraham, the God of Isaac, and the God
of Jacob." And Moses hid his face, for he was
afraid to look at God.

(Exodus 3:1-6)

OLY IS NOT WHAT GOD does; God doesn't act holy—He is holy, completely pure, true in every sense of the word. It is so important to know God is holy because it means all that He has said and done is holy too. I will tell you that there are things that have happened, as recorded in the Bible and as have occurred in my lifetime, that I do not understand. What I do know is that God, in His holiness, is perfect in all His ways, and those events that we don't understand are done or allowed by a God who is holy in all His ways. This is so important: We can know that because God is holy, His plans are holy. We can trust the one true, holy God—period!

> [5] *Trust in the LORD with all your heart;*
> *do not depend on your own understanding.*
> *(Proverbs 3:5, NLT)*

Arthur W. Pink said, "God's holiness is manifested in His works. 'The Lord is righteous in all his ways, and holy in all his works' (Psalm 145:17). Nothing but that which is excellent can proceed from Him. Holiness is the rule of all His actions."[39]

The world's view of God's holiness may have changed, but God has not. God's name and His character are thrown around like toys and often like a piece of trash. God is a holy God, and we cannot approach Him in any way other than through the finished work of Christ Jesus. We, as born-again believers in Jesus Christ, have to regain a deep recognition of God's holiness, a deep reverence—we need to get what Jesus meant when He taught us to pray, "Hallowed be your name" (Matthew 6:9).

When we know God is holy—pure and completely without error or failure—we can rest comfortably in the events of our lives. Knowing that God is holy is key to responding to the challenges of life. The words of the world around us are just throwaway words, hanging in the air for a moment and then gone. God has spoken, and His Word shall stand forever. The one and only holy God has spoken into your life, and you can stand on, build on, trust in, and rest your very life and eternity upon Him and what He has said.

> ³ Holy, holy, holy is the LORD of hosts;
> the whole earth is full of his glory!
>
> *(Isaiah 6:3)*

God has spoken clearly to us about holiness:

> ⁷ God has called us to live holy lives, not impure lives. ⁸ Therefore, anyone who refuses to live by these rules is not disobeying human teaching but is rejecting God, who gives his Holy Spirit to you.
>
> *(1 Thessalonians 4:7-8, NLT)*

Holiness is not an item on God's buffet of spiritual truths we can choose or pass over. He said if we don't pursue the holy life He calls us to, we are not rejecting man but rejecting God! Rejecting God is not a choice I want to make; do you want to reject God?

Holiness is not a plan of discipline for us; holiness is a great gift God wants us to embrace and enjoy in our lives. Holiness is a part of God's plan for you and for me.

> ⁹ For God saved us and called us to live a holy life. He did this, not because we deserved it, but because that was his plan from before the beginning of time—to show us his grace through Christ Jesus.
>
> *(2 Timothy 1:9, NLT)*

Since before the creation of the world, God's plan is for each of us to be in a dynamic love relationship with Him, living holy lives before Him. He carried out His part of the plan when He sent His only Son to die in my place and in your place and when He called us into a love relationship with Himself through Christ and led by the Holy Spirit. How can we say, "God, thanks for what You have done, but I want to bypass this 'holy' thing; it will be fine with me just to be a good religious person"? That God said, "Be holy," should be enough for us. Yet, we also are blessed and helped to know God's plan is not just holy; it is perfect for us and carried out with such deliberate love and sacrifice. Rejecting God's call to live holy lives is rejecting God and missing God's very best for each of us.

[16] You shall be holy, for I am holy.

(1 Peter 1:16)

We have only one answer to God's call to holiness: "Yes, Lord, yes to Your will and to Your way; yes, Lord yes with our whole heart we will obey." Any other response is to reject God.

Prayer focusing on God's holiness:

Heavenly Father, we rest in the knowledge that You are holy in all Your ways. We know that no matter what happens in and around us, it is all consistent with Your holiness. You are sovereign over this earth, and You have a plan to deal with the circumstances of this world. We can rest in the blessed assurance of who You are and what You are doing. You are God; You are holy, and all is well. We give thanks to You, our holy and loving God. Father, we know that You have called us to live holy lives. You have told us and shown us the way; in fact, You are the way! Lord, help us to have courage and love for You and get out of our spiritual rocking chair and live full tilt for Jesus—seeking to be holy in every way because You, the Lord our God, is holy. In Christ's name we pray.

Amen.

Chapter 19

God Is Fair

IT'S JUST NOT FAIR. NOT fair at all!" If you are a parent, you have heard this many times. If you are not a parent, then you remember saying this to your parents. You just know you were not treated fairly. The truth is, there are a lot of things people do to one another that are not fair. God is fair in all things and at all times. We have to know God is fair!

> [5] "But," some might say, "our sinfulness serves a good purpose, for it helps people see how righteous God is. Isn't it unfair, then, for him to punish us? (This is merely a human point of view.) [6] Of course not! If God were not entirely fair, how would he be qualified to judge the world?
>
> *(Romans 3:5-6, NLT)*

When our eyes first open in the morning, our first thoughts need to be about God—and we need to have right thoughts of God, to consciously think and know that:

- This is the day the Lord has made.
- God loves me.
- God is fair in all He does.
- God is holy.
- God is unchanging.
- God is sovereign.
- God is infinite, eternal, just, gracious...

When we know who God is, we know how the day will go, and we can say with great peace and joy, "Come what may this day; it is well with my soul." No matter what happens today, it is happening under the watch and care of a loving God, who is perfect in all of His ways and absolutely fair in all things.

One of the most dangerous and destructive things that can happen to a Christian is a spirit of bitterness. Recently, I dealt with a circumstance where I was starting to experience bitterness. I had never really been bitter in my life, but all of a sudden I was getting bitter because of circumstances over which I had no control. When we allow ourselves to become bitter or downhearted by outside circumstances, we are play-ing right into the hands of the enemy and failing to trust in God, who is fair in all circumstances. I was soon reminded that no matter what the circumstanc-es, nothing comes into my life that does not pass first through the hands of a loving, holy, and fair God. Instead of getting bitter (what I was getting bitter over was nothing in the grand scheme of life although it seemed large at the moment), I had to say. "Lord, I trust You, and in You all is well because I know You love me and You are fair in all Your ways."

Fairest Lord Jesus[40]

Fairest Lord Jesus,
Ruler of all nature,
O Thou of God and man the Son;
Thee will I cherish,
Thee will I honor,
Thou, my soul's glory, joy and crown.

Fair are the meadows,
Fairer still the woodlands,
Robed in the blooming garb of spring;
Jesus is fairer,
Jesus is purer,
Who makes the woeful heart to sing.

Fair is the sunshine,
Fairer still the moonlight
And all the twinkling, starry host;
Jesus shines brighter,
Jesus shines purer
Than all the angels heaven can boast.

Beautiful Savior,
Lord of all the nations,
Son of God and Son of man!
Glory and honor,
Praise, adoration,
Now and forevermore be Thine!

The whisper in your ear that you are not being treated fairly is not coming from the Holy Spirit. The enemy is trying to get you to believe you are being mistreated, that life is unfair to you and you need to take control. That thinking is not a move toward strength but rather toward weakness and destruction. The most powerful move we can make is to fall on our knees and cry out to God, who is fair in every way.

Prayer acknowledging that God is fair:

Lord, we acknowledge that You are the author of fairness; there is nothing fair apart from the fact You made it so. You are God, and You shine fair in all things. When I go out into the world today, no matter how difficult the circumstances that come my way, I can rest in the sure knowledge that You are fair in all things. Help me to know assuredly that my hope is not in the ways of the world but in the ways of God, and Your ways are exceedingly and abundantly fair. Thank You, God, for Your fairness in my life.

Amen.

Chapter 20

God Is Righteous

GOD IS IN CONTROL, AND He is righteous in all of His ways. This is challenging because there is much we do not understand about life. Every day we find ourselves asking, "Why, God?" We will at times continue to ask the question, but now we must move past the question to the knowledge: "God, no matter what happens today, no matter that I don't understand it, I know that You are righteous in all Your ways, and I can absolutely trust You!"

We must see God in His righteousness to come to the necessary and absolute reality and truth of our own unrighteousness. God is righteous and the source of all that is right; apart from Him, there is nothing righteous in us. We must completely abandon— yes, completely and finally abandon—any thought that we are righteous.

My Hope Is Built on Nothing Less[41]

My hope is built on nothing less
Than Jesus' blood and righteousness.
I dare not trust the sweetest frame,
But wholly lean on Jesus' name.

REFRAIN

On Christ the solid rock I stand,
all other ground is sinking sand;
all other ground is sinking sand.

When darkness veils His lovely face,
I rest on His unchanging grace.
In every high and stormy gale,
my anchor holds within the veil.

REFRAIN

His oath, His covenant, His blood,
support me in the whelming flood.
When all around my soul gives way,
He then is all my Hope and Stay.

REFRAIN

When He shall come with trumpet sound,
Oh may I then in Him be found.
Dressed in His righteousness alone,
faultless to stand before the throne.

REFRAIN

Have you ever given thought to how much time we spend being right or seeking to prove we are right? We spend an inordinate portion of our lives seeking to be right and proving that we are right. We want others to know we are right and they are wrong, that what we said was right (we were justified in acting as we did); in small, completely inconsequential things we want to make sure everyone knows we were right. The truth is, anything we do that is not solely for His glory and does not honor God is not right (and very few, if any, things in any of our lives meet that criteria). Likely there is nothing upon which we expend more time and energy than being right. We seek to be right above all else, yet we fail miserably. In vain do we seek to establish righteousness on our own, in ourselves. Self-righteousness is no righteousness! There is nothing we fail at more miserably than our efforts at self-righteousness.

God alone is righteous! Righteousness is a part of who God is, and God is the source of all righteousness. In the same way that God is light, God is righteous. We can no more achieve a state of righteousness apart from God than we can create light without relying on the light that is wholly from God.

What does God have to say about our efforts at self-righteousness?

^{10} *As the Scriptures say,*

"No one is righteous —
not even one.

^{11} *No one is truly wise;*
no one is seeking God.

¹² All have turned away;
all have become useless.

No one does good,
not a single one."

(Romans 3:10-12, NLT)

Where do you and I fit into the "no one is righteous, not even one"? That hits square in the face of our failed efforts to produce our own brand of righteousness. The whole truth is that none of us, nor any position we take, is righteous unless it is based on and rests wholly in Christ Jesus. Pursuit of righteousness, personally and professionally, has been a significant part of my life's efforts, but today I humbly bow and acknowledge God is righteous and beside Him is no other. On my very best days, and all other days too, I fall woefully short—my very best is like filthy rags in the presence of Almighty God. There is no more important lesson we can learn—at the moment we fully grasp our unrighteousness, we begin to see and understand God's perfect righteousness and our total dependence upon Him.

The failures in my life come from my failed efforts at self-righteousness. The reality is we all suffer this ill-advised course of pursuing our own brand of righteousness or self-righteousness—that is to say no righteousness. You have met with no better success than have I. Righteousness is a part of who God is, and it is ours only to the extent we have yielded our lives to Him through Christ Jesus as we are led by the Holy Spirit. The only righteousness in you and me is the righteousness that is of and from God.

¹⁷ Therefore, if anyone is in Christ, he is a new creation. The old has passed away; behold, the new has come. ¹⁸ All this is from God, who

through Christ reconciled us to himself and gave us the ministry of reconciliation; [19] that is, in Christ God was reconciling the world to himself, not counting their trespasses against them, and entrusting to us the message of reconciliation. [20] Therefore, we are ambassadors for Christ, God making his appeal through us. We implore you on behalf of Christ, be reconciled to God. [21] For our sake he made him to be sin who knew no sin, so that in him we might become the righteousness of God.

(2 Corinthians 5:17-21)

We need to know how important righteousness is to God. He is right, He is holy, and He has called us to the standard of righteousness. This is a picture of how we have done in response to God's call:

[18] For the wrath of God is revealed from heaven against all ungodliness and unrighteousness of men, who by their unrighteousness suppress the truth. [19] For what can be known about God is plain to them, because God has shown it to them. [20] For his invisible attributes, namely, his eternal power and divine nature, have been clearly perceived, ever since the creation of the world, in the things that have been made. So they are without excuse. [21] For although they knew God, they did not honor him as God or give thanks to him, but they became futile in their thinking, and their foolish hearts were darkened. [22] Claiming to be wise, they became fools, [23] and exchanged the glory of the immortal God for images resembling mortal man and birds and animals and creeping things.

(Romans 1:18-23)

We have no defense, and we have no valid excuse to offer for our unrighteousness. But we do have an answer, and that answer is Jesus. We just read this above, "He made him to be sin who knew no sin, so that in him we might become the righteousness of God" (2 Corinthians 5:21). We have one path to righteousness, and that path is a person—the person of Jesus Christ. Here is what Jesus has said about our journey:

> [1] "Let not your hearts be troubled. Believe in God; believe also in me. [2] In my Father's house are many rooms. If it were not so, would I have told you that I go to prepare a place for you? [3] And if I go and prepare a place for you, I will come again and will take you to myself, that where I am you may be also. [4] And you know the way to where I am going." [5] Thomas said to him, "Lord, we do not know where you are going. How can we know the way?" [6] Jesus said to him, "I am the way, and the truth, and the life. No one comes to the Father except through me. [7] If you had known me, you would have known my Father also. From now on you do know him and have seen him."
>
> *(John 14:1-7)*

God is righteous, and righteousness is His standard for our lives. When we begin to understand God's righteousness, then the answer to the question "Who do I say God is?" is in large part "God is righteous." Having settled in our mind once and for all that God is absolutely righteous and we are not, we can fully abandon our futile efforts at self-righteousness. We can enjoy the ultimate freedom of resting in the righteousness of Christ Jesus.

Paul explained that righteousness is a gift from God alone:

¹⁷ For if, because of one man's trespass, death reigned through that one man, much more will those who receive the abundance of grace and the free gift of righteousness reign in life through the one man Jesus Christ.

(Romans 5:17)

Knowing and embracing our unrighteousness is not a cause for lament but a foundation for celebration. In our recognition of God's righteousness, we are blessed with peace and freedom found nowhere else. Knowing God is righteous and we are not is the exact message of Jesus' very first words in His teaching we call "The Sermon on the Mount":

³ "Blessed are the poor in spirit, for theirs is the kingdom of heaven.

(Matthew 5:3)

To get a fuller sense of this verse, let's look at it in the Amplified Bible:

³ Blessed [spiritually prosperous, happy, to be admired] are the poor in spirit [those devoid of spiritual arrogance, those who regard themselves as insignificant], for theirs is the kingdom of heaven [both now and forever].

(Matthew 5:3, AMP)

Here is my word for it: When I understand that I have nothing to offer God, that I am totally and completely dependent upon Him, I begin to find the peace that passes all understanding in the finished work of Christ Jesus, who said on the cross, "It is finished." We need to be finished seeking our own righteousness and rest fully in His righteousness alone!

Prayer thanking God for His righteousness:

Heavenly Father, righteous God, You are righteous and I am not. Lord, help me to once and for all and forever lay aside the notion that there is any self-righteousness in me. Lord, I am poor, helpless, spiritually blind, and naked apart from Your saving grace. Lord, thank You for loving me so much that You sent Your only Son to become sin that I might become righteous in Him and before You—I am the righteousness of God in Christ Jesus, and for that I am eternally dependent and grateful. Thank You, righteous God, for making me right before you in Christ.

Amen.

Part Two

Who Are You in Christ?

Chapter 21

Who You Are in Christ

We have asked the question: Who do you say God is? There is another critical question, and simply put the question is: Who are you in Christ Jesus? Knowing who we are in Christ Jesus is the next step in the process of living out God's will for our lives. When we are born again into Christ Jesus as Lord and Savior, what does that mean for us? I want to know the answer to who I am in Christ Jesus!

> [13] I can do all things [which He has called me to do] through Him who strengthens and empowers me [to fulfill His purpose—I am self-sufficient in Christ's sufficiency; I am ready for anything and equal to anything through Him who infuses me with inner strength and confident peace].
> *(Philippians 4:13, AMP)*

The first thing I need to know about who I am in Christ is the power that is in His name. The name of Jesus is the most powerful weapon we have, and His name is irresistible and irrepressible:

> [9] *Therefore, God elevated him*
> *to the place of highest honor*
> *and gave him the name above all other names,*

*¹⁰ that at the name of Jesus every knee should bow,
in heaven and on earth and under the earth,*

*¹¹ and every tongue declare that Jesus Christ is Lord,
to the glory of God the Father.*
(Philippians 2:9-11, NLT)

Here is the biblical truth of who we are in Christ Jesus:

(1) In Christ, I am loved by the Father.

⁸ But God showed his great love for us by sending Christ to die for us while we were still sinners.
(Romans 5:8, NLT)

God speaks much about love, but right here He doesn't speak—He shows us His love. This is the original and authentic "love in"—a demonstration of God's great love. While I was still dead in my trespasses and sin, God sent His only Son Jesus to take my place and your place.

¹⁶ We know what real love is because Jesus gave up his life for us. So we also ought to give up our lives for our brothers and sisters.
(1 John 3:16, NLT)

God's demonstration of His love is the most powerful evidence we have of who we are in Christ.

¹⁶ For God so loved the world, that he gave his only Son, that whoever believes in him should not perish but have eternal life.
(John 3:16)

When we get up in the morning, it is imperative that we know God loves us—not just loves us but loves us this much:

> [17] Then Christ will make his home in your hearts as you trust in him. Your roots will grow down into God's love and keep you strong. [18] And may you have the power to understand, as all God's people should, how wide, how long, how high, and how deep his love is. [19] May you experience the love of Christ, though it is too great to understand fully. Then you will be made complete with all the fullness of life and power that comes from God.
>
> *(Ephesians 3:17-19, NLT)*

(2) *I am purchased at a price.*

How valuable you are! God sent His Son, His only Son, Jesus, for *you*! It has been said that if you were the only person who had ever been born, Jesus would have still come for you. You are valuable to the Father.

> [19] Don't you realize that your body is the temple of the Holy Spirit, who lives in you and was given to you by God? You do not belong to yourself, [20] for God bought you with a high price. So you must honor God with your body.
>
> *(1 Corinthians 6:19-20, NLT)*

We are so dearly loved by God that He has redeemed us by the precious blood of the Lamb.

> [18] For you know that God paid a ransom to save you from the empty life you inherited

from your ancestors. And it was not paid with mere gold or silver, which lose their value. [19] It was the precious blood of Christ, the sinless, spotless Lamb of God. [20] God chose him as your ransom long before the world began, but now in these last days he has been revealed for your sake.

(1 Peter 1:18-20, NLT)

There are many people who love to tell us who we are and who we are not. We have to see ourselves as we really are—in Christ. We are not just saved; we are precious in the eyes of God. It does not matter what anyone else says about you; the only opinion that really counts is God's.

(3) I am justified in Christ, declared innocent.

We are all under sin—there is no one who is without sin. If we claim to be without sin, we are lying (see Romans 3 and 1 John 1). We have no way of cleaning ourselves up; that is an impossibility. We stand guilty before God; without Christ we have no defense.

In Christ we are fully justified, declared by God to be innocent.

[16] Yet we know that a person is made right with God by faith in Jesus Christ, not by obeying the law. And we have believed in Christ Jesus, so that we might be made right with God because of our faith in Christ, not because we have obeyed the law. For no one will ever be made right with God by obeying the law.

(Galatians 2:16, NLT)

This is so important for us to know and to take in. We need to see spiritually that, for all who are in Christ, when we look in the mirror, a stamp on our forehead says, "Justified in Christ Jesus—I am the righteousness of God."

The old hymn says, "Jesus paid it all, all to Him I owe; sin had left a crimson stain, He washed it white as snow."[42] For us to live each day to the fullest, we have to know that we know we have been redeemed from our sins by Christ Jesus. We cannot be the faithful, alive, loving, Spirit-filled, and energetic people God put us here to be if we are dragging along a sack of our old sins. That is not from God. When God declares you innocent, you are innocent indeed.

> [8] If we say we have no sin, we deceive ourselves, and the truth is not in us. [9] If we confess our sins, he is faithful and just to forgive us our sins and to cleanse us from all unrighteousness. [10] If we say we have not sinned, we make him a liar, and his word is not in us.
>
> *(1 John 1:8-10)*

(4) I am, in Christ, given a clean conscience.

Do you bow to pray and hear a voice inside you saying something like "You might as well get up; you are no good; you are thinking bad thoughts"? That is not the voice of God. That is the voice of the accuser, Satan. He is most afraid when we are on our knees. The same is true when we open the Bible—we might hear that voice saying something like "You can't do those things; you are not good enough." Again, this is the voice of the enemy; don't listen to him.

We need to have a clean conscience, and here is one of the keys to having a clean conscience—the blood of Christ purifies our conscience.

> [14] how much more will the blood of Christ, who through the eternal Spirit offered himself without blemish to God, purify our conscience from dead works to serve the living God.
>
> *(Hebrews 9:14)*

We need to plaster this in our mind and conscience! In Romans 7, Paul was discussing how hard it is when we want to do the right thing and often do the opposite. He said he just could not understand it, and then at the end of chapter 7 he cried out and said, "Who is going to help with this?" His answer—Jesus! What he said next is something we need to never ever forget:

> [1] There is therefore now no condemnation for those who are in Christ Jesus.
>
> *(Romans 8:1)*

(5) I am, in Christ, separated from my sin.

We have to really begin to get excited about this truth. We are not just declared innocent; our sin is taken away. Did God send someone who works in the maintenance department in heaven to take away our sin? No, He sent Jesus Himself—His one and only Son—to take away my sin and yours!

> [29] The next day John saw Jesus coming toward him and said, "Look! The Lamb of God who takes away the sin of the world!"
>
> *(John 1:29, NLT)*

Corrie ten Boom once wrote that God casts our sins "into the deepest sea and a sign is put up that says, No Fishing Allowed." We do not go back and try to bring up that old sin—it is gone. We are separated from our sin. Satan wants us to go fishing and try to drag that sin back up because he knows it destroys our joy and he is greatly intimidated by joyful Christians who are celebrating their freedom in Christ.

We have to know God has put our sin far away.

> *12 He has removed our sins as far from us*
> *as the east is from the west.*
>
> *(Psalm 103:12, NLT)*

We are completely and permanently separated from our sin in Christ Jesus.

(6) I am, in Christ, at peace with God.

How many years, decades, centuries has the world tried to make peace treaties? More than we can possibly know! It is a fruitless venture—there is no peace apart from a right relationship with God. A right relationship with God is found only in Christ Jesus.

We worry about peace in our world. We worry about what will happen today; we worry about what will happen to us in the night. We will find something to worry about even when things are going great. Peace in our world and peace in our heart will only be found in a right relationship with God.

> *1 Therefore, since we have been made right in God's sight by faith, we have peace with God because of what Jesus Christ our Lord has done for us.*
>
> *(Romans 5:1, NLT)*

Worry is an anti-God state of mind. When I worry, when you worry, we are saying, "God cannot quite get this day done without me, and so I am going to worry things into a better state of being." How absurd. How disrespectful. Worry is possibly the most wasteful human emotion, and it is dishonoring to God.

The very best statement on this is found in the Apostle Paul's letter to the Church at Philippi:

> [4] Always be full of joy in the Lord. I say it again—rejoice! [5] Let everyone see that you are considerate in all you do. Remember, the Lord is coming soon.
>
> [6] Don't worry about anything; instead, pray about everything. Tell God what you need, and thank him for all he has done. [7] Then you will experience God's peace, which exceeds anything we can understand. His peace will guard your hearts and minds as you live in Christ Jesus.
>
> [8] And now, dear brothers and sisters, one final thing. Fix your thoughts on what is true, and honorable, and right, and pure, and lovely, and admirable. Think about things that are excellent and worthy of praise. [9] Keep putting into practice all you learned and received from me—everything you heard from me and saw me doing. Then the God of peace will be with you.
>
> *(Philippians 4:4-9, NLT)*

Paul laid it out perfectly:

- Be full of joy in Christ.
- Remember Jesus is coming back.
- Do not worry about anything.

• Tell God what your needs are and then leave it alone.

• When we do that, a peace deeper than anything we have known is ours.

When Paul said, "Always be full of joy in the Lord. I say it again—rejoice!" that is not a gentle suggestion—it is a command from the Lord! God is commanding us to rejoice in Him. By repeating this statement, God is showing us it is not only a command, but it is an important one!

Then Paul said, "Look, instead of worrying, once you have rejoiced in Him and talked to your Abba Father (your Daddy who loves you dearly) about your concerns and needs, once the peace of God is at work in you, there is a second step. Instead of worrying, think about these things:

• Truth (Jesus is truth)
• Honorable things (things that honor God)
• Right thoughts (found in God's Word)
• Things that are pure, lovely, and admirable (think about Jesus)

When we honor God in these ways, the peace of God will guard our hearts and minds in Christ Jesus.

(7) I am clothed in the righteousness of Christ.

"What should I wear today? Oh, I know. I will wear the righteousness of Christ." To get dressed properly is to receive and rest in the truth that when we are born again, we become right before God—we are clothed with Christ's righteousness. This is not by what we have done but by the finished work of Christ on the cross. Jesus became our sin for us so that we could become the righteousness of God.

> ²¹ God made him who had no sin to be sin for us, so that in him we might become the righteousness of God.
>
> *(2 Corinthians 5:21, NIV)*

We should never worry about how others see us; we need to pay attention to how God sees us. We are in the ultimate fashion that never changes or goes out of style—the righteousness of Christ.

(8) I am made new in Christ Jesus.

I am, in Christ, a brand-new person. Wow! When we truly get this, we understand one of the greatest truths and one of the greatest reassuring blessings found in all of God's promises. God has promised to you and to me:

> ¹⁶ So we have stopped evaluating others from a human point of view. At one time we thought of Christ merely from a human point of view. How differently we know him now! ¹⁷ This means that anyone who belongs to Christ has become a new person. The old life is gone; a new life has begun!
>
> *(2 Corinthians 5:16-17, NLT)*

This is a promise of God, and it is one we have to fully grasp and fiercely cling to. Instantly, when you are in Christ, you are brand new—and more—*the old is gone forever!* No matter what anyone else sees when they look at you, the person they used to know is gone. There is a new person inside those old clothes.

We have to begin to live out what God has done in us.

> [24] Put on your new nature, created to be like God—truly righteous and holy.
>
> *(Ephesians 4:24, NLT)*

How does all this happen? To be a new person, we must have a new birth. Jesus explained this very thing to Nicodemus:

> [3] Jesus answered him, "Truly, truly, I say to you, unless one is born again he cannot see the kingdom of God." [4] Nicodemus said to him, "How can a man be born when he is old? Can he enter a second time into his mother's womb and be born?" [5] Jesus answered, "Truly, truly, I say to you, unless one is born of water and the Spirit, he cannot enter the kingdom of God. [6] That which is born of the flesh is flesh, and that which is born of the Spirit is spirit. [7] Do not marvel that I said to you, 'You must be born again.' [8] The wind blows where it wishes, and you hear its sound, but you do not know where it comes from or where it goes. So it is with everyone who is born of the Spirit."
>
> *(John 3:3-8)*

In another place in John, we read this:

> [12] But to all who believed him and accepted him, he gave the right to become children of God. [13] They are reborn—not with a physical birth resulting from human passion or plan, but a birth that comes from God.
>
> *(John 1:12-13, NLT)*

We are not only a new person but the old person is gone. The life we live going forward is completely different. Here is the new life and what it looks like:

> [20] I have been crucified with Christ. It is no longer I who live, but Christ who lives in me. And the life I now live in the flesh I live by faith in the Son of God, who loved me and gave himself for me.
>
> *(Galatians 2:20)*

You and I are brand-new people in Christ Jesus. We need to live out what God has given us. What a great gift—a new life in Christ Jesus—there is nothing like it, nothing!

(9) I am seated with Christ.

When we are born again, we have the very best seat in the house; there is no better seat at any price. When we are born again, we are seated with Christ Jesus in the heavenly realms. In our old physical bodies, our feet are still touching the ground, but the spiritual newly born you is high (way higher than a kite).

> [6] For he raised us from the dead along with Christ and seated us with him in the heavenly realms because we are united with Christ Jesus.
>
> *(Ephesians 2:6, NLT)*

God does things in God-sized ways. He doesn't just clean us up a little; He cleans us up completely, dresses us in the righteousness of Jesus Christ, and gives us a seat with Christ in His presence.

Summary of Who You Are in Christ Jesus

Jesus told us that He was going to the Father and that we would do greater things than even what He did because of who we are in Christ Jesus. But no matter what He has done for us, our greatest joy must be that we are His. Look how He said this to His disciples:

> [17] The seventy-two returned with joy, saying, "Lord, even the demons are subject to us in your name!" [18] And he said to them, "I saw Satan fall like lightning from heaven. [19] Behold, I have given you authority to tread on serpents and scorpions, and over all the power of the enemy, and nothing shall hurt you. [20] Nevertheless, do not rejoice in this, that the spirits are subject to you, but rejoice that your names are written in heaven."
>
> *(Luke 10:17-20)*

In Christ you are:

- Loved by the Father
- Valuable to the Father, who gave a great price for you
- Justified before God
- Given a clean conscience
- Separated from your sin
- At peace with God
- Clothed with the righteousness of Christ
- Made completely new, the old you is gone
- Seated with Christ

We are called to belong to Christ, to live our lives fully surrendered to Him. We are no longer our own; we are His, which is far greater than anything we had or could ever have in this world. The things of this world do not and never could satisfy—just look around at those who have everything but don't have Jesus. They are always wanting more because what the world has given them cannot satisfy. But those who are in Christ have found the true peace and joy and love everyone seeks after but cannot find in things. In Christ, we have found and are continuing to find the peace that passes all understanding; the security that does not rise and fall with the markets; the hope that is rooted in the gracious, ever present, all holy, just, fair, and loving God who changes not.

Thou hast formed us for Thyself, and our hearts are restless till they find rest in Thee.
—Augustine

Prayer thanking God for who we are in Christ:

Father, thank You for loving us and sending your Son Jesus to die in our place; thank You that, in Christ, it is no longer we who live but Christ who lives in us. Help us, Lord, to live out the Christ who is in us by daily walking in the truth that, in Christ, we are loved by You, we are highly valued by You, we stand justified before You, we do not have to live in our past but have and maintain a clear conscience before You because we are separated from our sin as far as the east is from the west, and so we enjoy a deep, complete peace with You, O God, as we stand in Your presence dressed in the righteousness of Christ alone as new creations who are also seated with Christ Jesus in the heavens. We thank You, God, for who we are in Christ Jesus. It is in His precious name we pray.

Amen.

Part Three

What Will You Do with Jesus?

Chapter 22

How Then Shall We Live?

"Jesus paid it all, all to Him we owe; sin had left a crimson stain, He washed it white as snow!"[43] Jesus, very God of God, humbled Himself and came in the form of a baby and lived a sinless life; He humbled Himself to death on a cross that you and I may be reconciled to God and have abundant life. "Jesus paid it all, all to Him we owe." There now remains the one burning question: "What am I going to do with Jesus?"

In the words of Francis Schaeffer, "How should we then live?"[44] If you have met the living Lord Jesus Christ, you cannot leave Him alone; you are forced to choose: Shall we stay with Him or shall we go?

> [67] So Jesus said to the Twelve, "Do you want to go away as well?" [68] Simon Peter answered him, "Lord, to whom shall we go? You have the words of eternal life, [69] and we have believed, and have come to know, that you are the Holy One of God."
>
> (John 6:67-69)

Jesus, who is the word of life, has made a way for us and called us to Himself. Listen to what the Apostle Paul has written about the nature of our relationship with Christ:

> [5] through whom we have received grace and apostleship to bring about the obedience of faith for the sake of his name among all the nations, [6] including you who are called to *belong to Jesus Christ*.
>
> *(Romans 1:5-6, emphasis added)*

We must hear God loud and clear on this: He did not send His Son to save us so that we could sit idly by for decades waiting on the heavenly bus. He created us to belong to Jesus and to be like Jesus—to be Jesus' own:

> [29] For God knew his people in advance, and he chose them to become like his Son, so that his Son would be the firstborn among many brothers and sisters.
>
> *(Romans 8:29, NLT)*

God did not put us here to be puffed up in ourselves, taking great care of our reputation while doing nothing to proclaim Him. It is God's plan and purpose for you and for me to follow Jesus, to love Jesus, to follow in the path He has laid out for us by His wonderful example.

> [3] Don't be selfish; don't try to impress others. Be humble, thinking of others as better than yourselves. [4] Don't look out only for your own interests, but take an interest in others, too.
> [5] You must have the same attitude that Christ Jesus had.
> [6] Though he was God, he did not think of equality with God as something to cling to.

[7] Instead, he gave up his divine privileges; he took the humble position of a slave and was born as a human being.

When he appeared in human form, [8] he humbled himself in obedience to God and died a criminal's death on a cross.

(Philippians 2:3-8, NLT)

The life God has called us to in Christ Jesus has nothing to do with pumping up our status among fellow Christians or the world. His call on us has everything to do with us becoming less and Jesus becoming everything. When God calls us, He bids us to come and die to self and live for Him (see Luke 9:23). There is only one real life, and that is life in Christ Jesus.

Paul explained that, from a human point of view, he was kind of hot stuff in his day, but he quickly made it clear that the very things that are so important in the world are of no value in the Kingdom.

[7] I once thought these things were valuable, but now I consider them worthless because of what Christ has done. [8] Yes, everything else is worthless when compared with the infinite value of knowing Christ Jesus my Lord. For his sake I have discarded everything else, counting it all as garbage, so that I could gain Christ [9] and become one with him. I no longer count on my own righteousness through obeying the law; rather, I become righteous through faith in Christ. For God's way of making us right with himself depends on faith. [10] I want to know Christ and experience the mighty power that raised him from the dead. I want to suffer with him, sharing in his death, [11] so that one

way or another I will experience the resurrection from the dead!

(Philippians 3:7-11, NLT)

To follow Jesus Christ is a radically different way to live. Following Christ is not about having a regular pew and a long history with a local church (those are great things unless those things are "the thing"—then everything is wrong with them). Living in and for Christ Jesus is all about a life that is hidden in Him as you boldly proclaim by your daily life that Jesus is Savior and Lord in your life.

Many people picture Jesus as this mild-mannered, sweet guy who went around smiling at everyone and shuffling His feet in humility. Jesus is humble, and He is the best "good guy" ever, but hear what He says about following Him (note these are the words of Jesus to me and you):

[32] *Everyone who acknowledges me publicly* here on earth, I will also acknowledge before my Father in heaven. [33] But *everyone who denies me here on earth, I will also deny* before my Father in heaven.

[34] Don't imagine that I came to bring peace to the earth! I came not to bring peace, but a sword.

[35] "I have come to set a man against his father,
a daughter against her mother, and a daughter-in-law against her mother-in-law.

[36] Your enemies will be right in your own household!"

[37] *If you love your father or mother more than you love me, you are not worthy of being mine*; or if you love your son or daughter more than me, you are not worthy of being mine. [38] If you refuse to

take up your cross and follow me, you are not worthy of being mine. [39] *If you cling to your life, you will lose it; but if you give up your life for me, you will find it.*

(*Matthew 10:32-39, NLT, emphasis added*)

What does it mean to acknowledge Jesus? For sure, it means that we are living the way He called us to live. He does not mean we can say a little prayer when we are alone and then live selfish, worldly lives and count on Him to acknowledge us before the Father. We are not speaking here of works earning us a spot in heaven; what Jesus is saying is "If you really belong to Me, you are going to acknowledge Me by your words and your actions; your very life is going to declare that you are Mine."

Jesus said if we belong to Him, He will be the priority in our life. We are going to love Jesus above all other people; we are going to love Him so much that we will lose life as we once knew it and give ourselves fully to Him. We are going to let reputation and worldly goods slip away, and Christ will be on the throne of our hearts—not so we can make things right with God but because God has made things right with us through Jesus, whom we have trusted fully. We have said to Jesus, "I am fully in, fully trusting in You, Lord Jesus, and Your finished work; my life is now in You, Lord."

Jesus spoke these words to His disciples, and they also apply to you and me:

[24] Then Jesus told his disciples, "*If anyone* would come after me, let him *deny himself* and *take up his cross* and *follow me*. [25] For *whoever would save his life will lose it*, but *whoever loses his life for my sake will find it*. [26] For what will it

profit a man if he gains the whole world and forfeits his soul? Or what shall a man give in return for his soul?"

(*Matthew 16:24-26, emphasis added*)

When Jesus said, "*If anyone* would come after [follow] me," He certainly was including you and me! He is saying to us, "If you are in Christ, if you really are a born-again Christian, you will . . ."

• **Deny yourself:** Quit living selfishly by the flesh and live according to the Spirit who lives in you. (The Holy Spirit lives in us if, in fact, we belong to Christ.)

• **Take up your cross:** What did the cross represent to Jesus? Dying to self. Saying, as Jesus did in the garden, "Nevertheless, not my will, but yours, be done" (Luke 22:42). To take up your cross is to daily offer yourself to God, saying, "Your will, Your way, Your time, Father, into Your hands I surrender my life, all that I have and all that I am" (see Romans 12:1-2; Galatians 2:20).

• **Follow Me:** To follow Jesus is to live a life where your daily plan is to trust and obey God. This does not mean "quit your job and go to some foreign land."[45] He is telling us to follow Him in trusting God right where we are: in our job, in our home, in our community. If we are teaching, then we teach as unto the Lord; if we are welding, we weld as unto the Lord; if we are a painter, then paint as unto the Lord; if we are a stay-at-home parent, then parent and care for the home as unto the Lord. He is telling us to live out Proverbs 3:5-6: "Trust in the LORD with all your heart, and do not lean on your own understanding. In all your ways acknowledge him, and he will make straight your paths." If you give your life to Him, you will find clear direction and purpose, with passion and joy. You will begin to understand and live out the abundant life Jesus came to give you. You will experience the process of growing toward being a one-hundred-fold Christian.

Paul was saying, "I have given up everything of worldly value in my life, and my focus is on Jesus! Paul was saying, "All that stuff that the world thinks is important, I don't care at all about that. What I do know is I want to know Jesus and everything about Him, and the only way to do that is to know Him as a crucified Savior. I want to be like Him in all things, that I might follow Him in many ways." Paul said, "I even want to know and experience the sufferings that Christ went through."

A Christ-centered life is not one preceded by a positive answer to: Is this safe? Is this the best time? Is this acceptable to all those who love me? A Christ-centered life is one where the only thing is simply this: full surrender to the will and way of God. We don't surrender with conditions of where, when, how, or any other earthly concerns. The answer to what am I going to do with Jesus is either: His way, His time, His place or not at all.

Prayer on how we shall live our lives:

Lord Jesus, help me, help us, to live our lives wholly for You. Help us to die to ourselves, forgetting our agenda and living for Your agenda; to set aside our priorities and to live out Your priorities. Father, we pray that we would daily die to self and take up our cross and follow Jesus in our thoughts, words, and actions. Lord, help us to live Christ–centered lives, to stand and live upon the Rock that is Jesus. It is in His holy, precious, and sweet name that we pray.

Amen.

Chapter 23

Living by the Spirit

WE CANNOT LIVE THE LIFE Jesus calls us to in our own strength and with our own abilities. If people were able to live lives that were pleasing and acceptable to God in their own strength, God would not have sent His only Son to die. To have and live the abundant life Jesus promises, we must have Jesus Himself—it is His reason for coming, that you and I may have life.

> [7] So Jesus again said to them, "Truly, truly, I say to you, I am the door of the sheep. [8] All who came before me are thieves and robbers, but the sheep did not listen to them. [9] I am the door. If anyone enters by me, he will be saved and will go in and out and find pasture. [10] The thief comes only to steal and kill and destroy. I came that they may have life and have it abundantly."
>
> (John 10:7-10)

Jesus is the door into real life. There is no other door, yet Jesus told His disciples they needed a Helper. Listen to what He said about the Helper:

> [4] I did not say these things to you from the beginning, because I was with you. [5] But now I am going to him who sent me, and none of you asks me, "Where are you going?" [6] But because I have said these things to you, sorrow has filled your heart. [7] Nevertheless, I tell you the truth: it is to your advantage that I go away, for if I do not go away, the Helper will not come to you. But if I go, I will send him to you. [8] And when he comes, he will convict the world concerning sin and righteousness and judgment: [9] concerning sin, because they do not believe in me; [10] concerning righteousness, because I go to the Father, and you will see me no longer; [11] concerning judgment, because the ruler of this world is judged.
>
> *(John 16:4-11)*

> [6] So when they had come together, they asked him, "Lord, will you at this time restore the kingdom to Israel?" [7] He said to them, "It is not for you to know times or seasons that the Father has fixed by his own authority. [8] But you will receive power when the Holy Spirit has come upon you, and you will be my witnesses in Jerusalem and in all Judea and Samaria, and to the end of the earth." [9] And when he had said these things, as they were looking on, he was lifted up, and a cloud took him out of their sight.
>
> *(Acts 1:6-9)*

The disciples had been with Jesus daily for about three years. They were not reading about Jesus; He had spoken with them personally every day. They had been right there and seen Jesus heal countless people—the blind regained sight, the lame walked, and the deaf could hear. They had personally seen Jesus raise people from the dead. Yet Jesus said to them, "Don't go anywhere or try to do anything without the Helper," meaning the Holy Spirit.

So, what about you and me? Can we live this life God has called us to without the Holy Spirit? No! Where do we get this Holy Spirit? If you are in Christ, then the Holy Spirit is in you.

> [1] So now there is no condemnation for those who belong to Christ Jesus. [2] And because you belong to him, the power of the life-giving Spirit has freed you from the power of sin that leads to death. [3] The law of Moses was unable to save us because of the weakness of our sinful nature. So God did what the law could not do. He sent his own Son in a body like the bodies we sinners have. And in that body God declared an end to sin's control over us by giving his Son as a sacrifice for our sins. [4] He did this so that the just requirement of the law would be fully satisfied for us, who no longer follow our sinful nature but instead follow the Spirit.
>
> [5] Those who are dominated by the sinful nature think about sinful things, but those who are controlled by the Holy Spirit think about things that please the Spirit. [6] So letting your sinful nature control your mind leads to death. But letting the Spirit control your mind leads to life and peace. [7] For the sinful nature is always hostile to God. It never did obey God's

laws, and it never will. [8] That's why those who are still under the control of their sinful nature can never please God.

[9] But you are not controlled by your sinful nature. You are controlled by the Spirit if you have the Spirit of God living in you. (And remember that those who do not have the Spirit of Christ living in them do not belong to him at all.) [10] And Christ lives within you, so even though your body will die because of sin, the Spirit gives you life because you have been made right with God. [11] The Spirit of God, who raised Jesus from the dead, lives in you. And just as God raised Christ Jesus from the dead, he will give life to your mortal bodies by this same Spirit living within you.

[12] Therefore, dear brothers and sisters, you have no obligation to do what your sinful nature urges you to do. [13] For if you live by its dictates, you will die. But if through the power of the Spirit you put to death the deeds of your sinful nature, you will live. [14] For all who are led by the Spirit of God are children of God.

(Romans 8:1-14, NLT)

What does this mean on a practical level? How do I live by the Spirit today and not by the flesh? First, we have to be born again.

[1] Now there was a man of the Pharisees named Nicodemus, a ruler of the Jews. [2] This man came to Jesus by night and said to him, "Rabbi, we know that you are a teacher come from God, for no one can do these signs that you do unless God is with him." [3] Jesus answered him, "Truly, truly, I say to you, unless

one is born again he cannot see the kingdom of God." [4] Nicodemus said to him, "How can a man be born when he is old? Can he enter a second time into his mother's womb and be born?" [5] Jesus answered, "Truly, truly, I say to you, unless one is born of water and the Spirit, he cannot enter the kingdom of God. [6] That which is born of the flesh is flesh, and that which is born of the Spirit is spirit. [7] Do not marvel that I said to you, 'You must be born again.' [8] The wind blows where it wishes, and you hear its sound, but you do not know where it comes from or where it goes. So it is with everyone who is born of the Spirit."

(John 3:1-8)

We must be born again. Okay, so how does that happen?

[16] For God so loved the world, that he gave his only Son, that whoever believes in him should not perish but have eternal life.

(John 3:16)

God loves us and made a way for us to be saved by believing in Jesus and His finished work. Jesus' final words on the cross were "It is finished."

[28] After this, Jesus, knowing that all was now finished, said (to fulfill the Scripture), "I thirst." [29] A jar full of sour wine stood there, so they put a sponge full of the sour wine on a hyssop branch and held it to his mouth. [30] When Jesus had received the sour wine, he said, "It is finished," and he bowed his head and gave up his spirit.

(John 19:28-30)

Jesus was simply saying He had finished His work of accomplishing salvation—He had paid our sin debt in full. He made a way for us to come to the Father through the finished work of the Son. Jesus also said that He is the way, the truth, and the life and no man came to the Father except through Him.

> [1] "Let not your hearts be troubled. Believe in God; believe also in me. [2] In my Father's house are many rooms. If it were not so, would I have told you that I go to prepare a place for you? [3] And if I go and prepare a place for you, I will come again and will take you to myself, that where I am you may be also. [4] And you know the way to where I am going." [5] Thomas said to him, "Lord, we do not know where you are going. How can we know the way?" [6] Jesus said to him, "I am the way, and the truth, and the life. No one comes to the Father except through me. [7] If you had known me, you would have known my Father also. From now on you do know him and have seen him."
>
> *(John 14:1-7)*

God has made a way; the way is Jesus. Jesus has done all of the work for us to be saved, and salvation is a gift to us from God. How do we receive this gift of life from God?

> [1] And you were dead in the trespasses and sins [2] in which you once walked, following the course of this world, following the prince of the power of the air, the spirit that is now at work in the sons of disobedience— [3] among whom we all once lived in the passions of our flesh, carrying out the desires of the body and the mind, and

were by nature children of wrath, like the rest of mankind. [4]But God, being rich in mercy, because of the great love with which he loved us, [5]even when we were dead in our trespasses, made us alive together with Christ—by grace you have been saved— [6]and raised us up with him and seated us with him in the heavenly places in Christ Jesus, [7]so that in the coming ages he might show the immeasurable riches of his grace in kindness toward us in Christ Jesus. [8]For by grace you have been saved through faith. And this is not your own doing; it is the gift of God, [9]not a result of works, so that no one may boast. [10]For we are his workmanship, created in Christ Jesus for good works, which God prepared beforehand, that we should walk in them.

(Ephesians 2:1-10)

When we are, by grace alone, through faith alone, in Christ alone, born again, the Holy Spirit resides in us. The Holy Spirit makes His home in all who are in Christ.

[9]But you are not controlled by your sinful nature. You are controlled by the Spirit if you have the Spirit of God living in you. (And remember that those who do not have the Spirit of Christ living in them do not belong to him at all.) [10]And Christ lives within you, so even though your body will die because of sin, the Spirit gives you life because you have been made right with God. [11]The Spirit of God, who raised Jesus from the dead, lives in you. And just as God raised Christ Jesus from the dead, he will give life to your mortal bodies by this same Spirit living within you.

(Romans 8:9-11, NLT)

Here is where we must make a firm decision: Do we live by the Holy Spirit who is in us or by the way of the flesh that is still with us and will be with us as long as we are in this physical life? I will now state an opinion, but it is an opinion based on many experiences, most of which are failures I have been guilty of. The Holy Spirit is in all who are in Christ, but the Holy Spirit is not always in control of all who are in Christ.

Is your life controlled by the Holy Spirit of God or by your flesh, which is influenced by the spirit of this world, the enemy? The Holy Spirit is God, but the Holy Spirit is—to use words we understand—a person. Because the Holy Spirit is in a Christian doesn't mean that the Christian has a love relationship with the Holy Spirit. Many Christians share a home but do not enjoy a dedicated, growing, and healthy love relationship. Relationships must be developed and nurtured. The Holy Spirit wants to guide us, and He is ready and willing and more than able to guide us into all truth. We have to be listening and ready, willing and able to hear the Holy Spirit; we have to develop a listening ear to the Holy Spirit's voice. We cannot be led by the Spirit if we are not lovingly listening to Him with a heart desiring to obey.

The Holy Spirit is God, the Holy Spirit of God. Where do we personally encounter God most readily and frequently? The Bible is the Word of God, and it is the resource we turn to most to hear what God has to say. We will not hear if we do not listen. We are not listening if we are not spending committed, focused regular and frequent time in the Word of God. The Word of God gives us the road signs the Holy Spirit uses to guide us. If we drive down the highway, thinking we know the way, and ignore the signs, we will miss the turn. When we are not spending time in the Word, guided by the Holy Spirit, we miss the turns in life.

Reading the Bible daily is not just a God-honoring thing; it is also very self-serving. Unless we feed ourselves daily from the Word of God, we will be spiritually anemic and unable to hear the Spirit speaking to us. I firmly believe that I was saved (born again) when I was twelve. Since then there have been a number of tragic failures by me. It is my understanding and belief that I was saved and the Holy Spirit resided in me (since age twelve), but I tuned Him out and turned Him off and started navigating my own course, and I wound up just where you would expect—crashed and burned (tragically many others were with me and I caused great damage to the witness God wanted to have in me and through me). That same Holy Spirit, in a way I don't understand and cannot explain, through the haze of alcohol, told me at about 7:30 a.m. on August 7, 2008, "Your life is not going to end this way." In spite of all those failures, I was still reading God's Word on a regular basis, so there was a little bit of spiritual hearing still left in me—and I heard. Oh, how much better it would be for me and for many if I had not lost my spiritual hearing for so long and in such drastic ways.[46] Here is my point: Because the Holy Spirit resides in us does not necessarily mean we are being led by the Spirit. One of the keys to being led by the Spirit is to spend time daily in the Word of God, being led by the Spirit of God to the person of God. If we don't have this ongoing and growing relationship with the Holy Spirit, then the flesh has more sway—and the way of the flesh is always contrary to the way of the Spirit. We have to be in God's Word daily, seeking God's road signs for our lives.

Daily committed and focused prayer time is another absolute necessity for the leadership of the Holy Spirit to be effective in our lives. How much of a burden was it for us to spend time with and offer adoration to our first girlfriend or boyfriend? Who has to encourage us to ooh and aah over our newborn children and even more so grandchildren? No one! We don't have to be convinced to love them, spend time with them, or say wonderful things to them. Why do we have such a hard time getting into a real dynamic and wonderful prayer relationship with our Creator? Almighty God, who is described in some detail in Part One of this book, is present and actively listening and speaking in prayer. We need to get up and run to our prayer closets with great anticipation daily and frequently.

Once we have heard and answered Jesus' question "But who do you say that I am?" (Matthew 16:15) according to the truth God has revealed to us in Scripture, and once we have come to know who we are in Christ, we have no problem wanting to talk to God. He is not a God far away; He is in your prayer closet. He is not a God who just might be interested in you; He is the one and only God, our Creator, the One who loves us so much He sent His only Son to die in our place. He is not a God who may want to do good things for you; He wants to do great and wonderful things for us—in fact, He wants to do immeasurably more than you and I can even imagine (see Ephesians 3:20). Very God of God, greater than anyone or anything, is here. He is listening. He is able to answer, and He wants to answer. Can we even imagine not talking to Him? Can you imagine having some celebrity come and stay at your home and you not spending much time talking with them? If your guest were open to such, you would stay up all night visiting with them. God, who created us, loves us, and has a plan for us now and in eternity is with us twenty-four hours a day, seven days a week, yet we have problems making time to speak to Him.

Oh, we will jump into a conversation with God real quick when things start going awry. We are quick to ask when we have a problem, but what about just talking with God daily, thanking Him for just being Him and for all the ways He has sustained us to this very moment—why do we struggle so hard against such a conversation? Here it is in a nutshell: We have to listen to and speak with God; nothing is more important and nothing is sweeter than a talk with Almighty God, who loves us and actually listens to what we say. He wants to answer our prayers with His plan for blessing us beyond our imagination. I cannot imagine us not talking with Him frequently!

What is it like to live and be led by the Holy Spirit as opposed to being led by the flesh? Living by the Spirit is the easiest way we could ever live. Every day we fight our way through battles that are often completely overwhelming mentally, physically, emotionally, financially, relationally, and personally. This kind of struggle-dominated, anxiety-ridden life is completely unnecessary and contrary to God's will for us. God wants us to live lives of peace—not that it will all be easy (it will not!)—and He has commanded us to live life rejoicing and given us a means to accomplish a joyful and peaceful life. His plan is for us to be led by the Holy Spirit.

> [5] Those who are dominated by the sinful nature think about sinful things, but those who are controlled by the Holy Spirit think about things that please the Spirit. [6] So letting your sinful nature control your mind leads to death. But letting the Spirit control your mind leads to life and peace.
>
> (Romans 8:5-6, NLT)

We have the choice today—which way will we live? Will we live the old way, led by the flesh directing us into error and calamity? Or will we live according to the Holy Spirit? God has given us Himself—the Holy Spirit—to live in us. I don't want to live my way anymore. I want to live by the Spirit, and so must we all if we are to live the life God put us here to live.

Listen to how Paul described this dichotomy of life my way versus life in the Holy Spirit:

[16] So I say, let the Holy Spirit guide your lives. Then you won't be doing what your sinful nature craves. [17] The sinful nature wants to do evil, which is just the opposite of what the Spirit wants. And the Spirit gives us desires that are the opposite of what the sinful nature desires. These two forces are constantly fighting each other, so you are not free to carry out your good intentions. [18] But when you are directed by the Spirit, you are not under obligation to the law of Moses.

[19] When you follow the desires of your sinful nature, the results are very clear: sexual immorality, impurity, lustful pleasures, [20] idolatry, sorcery, hostility, quarreling, jealousy, outbursts of anger, selfish ambition, dissension, division, [21] envy, drunkenness, wild parties, and other sins like these. Let me tell you again, as I have before, that anyone living that sort of life will not inherit the Kingdom of God.

[22] But the Holy Spirit produces this kind of fruit in our lives: love, joy, peace, patience, kindness, goodness, faithfulness, [23] gentleness, and self-control. There is no law against these things!

[24] Those who belong to Christ Jesus have nailed the passions and desires of their sinful

nature to his cross and crucified them there.
²⁵ Since we are living by the Spirit, let us follow the Spirit's leading in every part of our lives.
²⁶ Let us not become conceited, or provoke one another, or be jealous of one another.

(Galatians 5:16-26, NLT)

Wow, let me see—do I want constant fighting, jealousy, envy, anger, lust . . . or do I want to live a life of love, joy, peace, patience? How in the world could we ever miss this and go back down those old dead-end roads? We will not miss it if we do these simple things:

- Wake up praising God for who He is
- Give the firstfruits of every day to spending time with the Lord in prayer and reading and meditating on the Word of God
- Ask God every day for a fresh infilling of the Holy Spirit
- Offer ourselves to God as living sacrifices
- Pray daily for the Holy Spirit's guidance, leadership, and control in our lives
- Seek God's guidance frequently during the day when we catch ourselves trying to wrestle the wheel back from the Holy Spirit and surrender again and again

Prayer for a life filled and led by the Holy Spirit:

Heavenly Father, we are Your dearly loved children, and we thank You so much for the precious gift of the blessed Holy Spirit. Pour out Your Spirit upon us afresh and anew right now. Help us, Lord, to daily seek You in Your Word, in prayer, and in meditation on Your Word; help us, Lord, to listen attentively to the Holy Spirit as we pray and read Your Word, as we encounter others throughout the day so that we would know what to say, where to go, and what to do so that we live to-day and every day led by the Spirit rather than by the flesh. Lord, help us to be humble enough to readily con-fess when we get in the flesh, to seek forgiveness for our leaving the known and true path, and to surrender again and again to You. Lord, if we have to surrender every hour of every day, help us to know it is Your will and Your way, and it is a huge blessing to us to live life controlled by the Holy Spirit in our thoughts, words, and actions. Lord, thank You for the grace that enables us to know and seek and love the Holy Spirit. May this be our daily reality in Jesus' precious name.

Amen.

Conclusion

GOD BIDS US TO COME and die! This is not a call for just a few especially religious people; this is God's call upon each of our lives. He says, "If *anyone* would come after me . . ." (Matthew 16:24)! Does the evidence of how we live our lives today convict us of being true followers of Jesus Christ? This is all about God. Honoring God first and foremost by our lives is the issue here. We do not honor God when we live satisfied with a little religion; in fact, nothing could dishonor God more than for us to think we can live a Christian life at a lukewarm temperature. Jesus said,

> ¹⁵ I know all the things you do, that you are neither hot nor cold. I wish that you were one or the other! ¹⁶ But since you are like lukewarm water, neither hot nor cold, I will spit you out of my mouth!
>
> *(Revelation 3:15-16, NLT)*

What is our proper response to God who, having no need whatsoever for you or me, has given His all for us to be in a dynamic love relationship? He bids us come and die:

> 23 And Jesus answered them, "The hour has come for the Son of Man to be glorified. 24 Truly, truly, I say to you, unless a grain of wheat falls into the earth and dies, it remains alone; but if it dies, it bears much fruit. 25 Whoever loves his life loses it, and whoever hates his life in this world will keep it for eternal life. 26 If anyone serves me, he must follow me; and where I am, there will my servant be also. If anyone serves me, the Father will honor him."
>
> *(John 12:23-26)*

There is no such thing as being a partial Christian. We are either following Jesus or following the enemy. Jesus said, "If you want to follow Me, you must turn from your selfish ways, take up your cross, and follow Me." He doesn't promise us an easy way; in fact, He specifically told us that our way in this world will be hard:

> 33 I have told you all this so that you may have peace in me. Here on earth you will have many trials and sorrows. But take heart, because I have overcome the world.
>
> *(John 16:33, NLT)*

We are only here for a few years, which seem more like a few days. John Newton, in the song "Amazing Grace," wrote, "When we've been there ten thousand years, bright shining as the sun. We've no less days to sing God's praise, than when we first begun." Our time here is precious and short; may we grasp and live out Christ's call to die to self and follow Him.

Finally, the Apostle Paul said it so well in his letter to the Romans:

> [18] Yet what we suffer now is nothing compared to the glory he will reveal to us later. [19] For all creation is waiting eagerly for that future day when God will reveal who his children really are.
>
> *(Romans 8:18-19, NLT)*

May we relish the day in which we now live and draw breath with great passion, purpose, and joy, and, like Paul, may we look forward to the future glory when Jesus comes back. I pray He finds us on fire for Him, seeking to live the crucified life in Christ Jesus.

Postscript

THIS MORNING, AFTER FINISHING THE conclusion and laying the manuscript down, I went for a long run.[47] My usual path involves the Biloxi Bay Bridge, and this is what I saw on that bridge: a motorcycle doing approximately one hundred miles per hour, going up the incline with his front tire in the air and his head in the wind. I do not recommend riding your bike like that, but it is a perfect picture of how to live radically for Jesus Christ. It is the picture of how I would like, by God's grace, to finish my race and the exact picture of the disciples who laid down their lives to follow Jesus. Lord, help us to throw ourselves at the foot of the cross and live all out for Jesus.

Appendix A

Suggested Resources for Study:

THE HOLY BIBLE IS ABSOLUTELY required. The Internet allows us to have access to many different versions at no cost other than the cost of connecting. I strongly recommend the ESV and Amplified versions. I also enjoy and believe I have been helped by the NIV, NLT, and of course the KJV.

Memorizing verses of Scripture and even whole chapters and books is a tremendous tool for growing and maturing in Christ.

I suggest a continual daily reading of:

Psalms based on the day of the month: On the first day of the month, read Psalms 1, 31, 61, 91, 121 and do the same for each day of the month; every month you will read through the entire book of Psalms. If your time is constricted, then read a psalm a day matching the day of the month, and in the second month do the same but go up thirty (for the second month the first day you read Psalm 31, then 32, and so on). Do the same for the third month until you complete the book, and then begin again.

Proverbs: Read the chapter of Proverbs that corresponds to the day of the month.

In all this reading, do not hurry. Read carefully, meditatively, seeing and noting in your journal what God is showing you, questions you see there, commands of God, warnings from God. Then bring your questions before God and ask Him to guide you into all truth.

Read from the Old Testament and the New Testament daily. Yet may we please note that God is more interested in us really getting what we read than in us trying to impress Him or anyone with how much we read. Reading through the Bible in a year is a great goal, but I believe God would rather have us read one chapter in a week and fully get it than to get through many chapters but not hear what He is saying. *The whole purpose of reading and thinking on Scripture is to meet God, to come to know God better, to know ourselves, and to see our desperate need for God!* Reading the Bible as if it is literature is not God's goal for us in His Word. The Bible is the Word of God—dynamic and alive and ready to transform us into Christlikeness as the Spirit of God guides us.

ALSO EXPLORE THE WRITINGS OF:

A. W. Tozer
John R. W. Stott
Thomas à Kempis
C. S. Lewis
Timothy Keller
Jim Cymbala
Eric Metaxas
Andrew Murray
George Müller
Corrie ten Boom
Dr. Charles Stanley
Charles Spurgeon
Dr. Billy Graham
Francis Frangipane
Terry Teykl
Kenneth Boa (praying Scripture back
to God)
Robert J. Morgan

Worship is another key practice that helps prepare our hearts as we seek the Lord. We need to have great old hymnbooks and books of the praise and worship songs of today by our side in addition to our Bibles. Hymnbooks are the greatest tools to lead us into daily worship, which helps prepare our hearts for prayer and is itself prayer. God inhabits the praises of His people; no matter what is going on in your life, when you begin to praise God, the blessings of God are poured out afresh and anew. Singing hymns and worship songs daily is a must as a part of our daily seeking after God!

Endnotes

INTRODUCTION

1. Rudyard Kipling, in his *Barrack-room ballads*, 1892: "Oh, East is East, and West is West, and never the twain shall meet."

CHAPTER 1: KNOWING AND TRUSTING GOD

2. "Good Good Father," recorded by Chris Tomlin, written by Pat Barrett and Tony Brown, copyright 2014 Capitol CMG Paragon.
3. Galatians 2:20 says, "I have been crucified with Christ. It is no longer I who live, but Christ who lives in me. And the life I now live in the flesh I live by faith in the Son of God, who loved me and gave himself for me."
4. It is an absolute spiritual reality (see 2 Corinthians 5:17) that when we are saved, we are transformed. The experiencing of those changes is worked out daily in our lives for the rest of our lives.
5. Let me be clear. I deeply regret my failures. My failures came from my sinful choices. God hates sin. The point is, in spite of and in the midst of my failures, God is at work to accomplish His plan.

6. "My Hope Is Built on Nothing Less," Edward Mote, 1834.

Chapter 3: Knowing God Reveals Our Purpose in Life

7. While working on this book, I sensed God wanted me to step down from my job as a senior status judge in the state of Mississippi. Many people have asked, "What are you going to do next?" My answer is simply, "I am trusting God to direct my paths; He will show me at the right time. Right now my job is to trust and obey."

8. A. W. Tozer, *The Worship-Driven Life*, James L. Snyder, ed. (Oxford: Monarch Books, 2008), 10.

9. Ken Curtis, "Priceless Wisdom from Bro. Lawrence," Christianity.com, http://www.christianity.com/church/church-history/timeline/1601-1700/priceless-wisdom-from-bro-lawrence-11630063.html.

10. Westminster Larger Catechism (Edinburgh, Scotland: 1648).

Chapter 4: Who God Is in Himself

11. God is God, and man is not. We cannot fully know God as long as we are in these bodies. One day we will see Him as He really is, but for today God has given us the full revelation of Himself that we need to know and love and worship Him.

12. I have seen a number of different viewpoints on the number and specifics of what we here call the "attributes of God." I do not claim this to be an exhaustive listing of God's attributes; there is not enough paper or books in the world for such

a list. These are the ones that I have heard from God on.

13. It is we who leave; God has been there all along. God never goes anywhere; He is already everywhere, the great "I Am."

CHAPTER 5: GOD IS ONE: FATHER, SON, AND HOLY SPIRIT

14. There are many such human efforts to put the Trinity into words; they are all well meaning and often well thought-out but nevertheless fall far short of even an adequate explanation of the fullness of the unexplainable God.

15. Tozer is quoting Saint Anselm of Canterbury, a Benedictine monk, philosopher, and theologian from the eleventh century. Anselm was Archbishop, Doctor of the Church. Celebration of Feast Day is April 21. Taken from Father Joseph Vann, ed., *Lives of Saints* (J. J. Crawley, 1954).

16. A. W. Tozer, *The Knowledge of the Holy* (New York: HarperCollins, 1961), 17, 20.

17. Tozer, *Knowledge of the Holy*, 20.

18. Nicene Creed, http://www.usccb.org/beliefs-and-teachings/what-we-believe/.

19. Nicene Creed.

20. Tozer, *Knowledge of the Holy*, chapter 4.

CHAPTER 6: GOD IS LIGHT

21. H. D. M. Spence-Jones, ed., *1 John* (London; New York: Funk & Wagnalls Company, 1909), 3–4.

22. Spence-Jones, *1 John*, 3–4.

23. Adam Clarke, *First John* (1835), electronic ed. (Albany, OR: Ages Software, 1999). 1 Jn 4:8.
24. Spiros Zodhiates, *The Complete Word Study Dictionary: New Testament*, electronic ed. (Chattanooga, TN: AMG Publishers, 2000).
25. This does not refer to a spouse or a child being abused or any other similar abuse. I am referring here to the normal give and take in daily life when people offend us.
26. The sovereignty of God is addressed in a later chapter.

CHAPTER 9: GOD IS ETERNAL

27. *Simultaneous* is a word that relates to time and so is not adequate here, but it is what we have to work with.

CHAPTER 10: GOD IS ALMIGHTY

28. "Awesome God," Rich Mullins, 1988.

CHAPTER 12: GOD IS OMNIPRESENT

29. "He Is Here," performed by the Gaither Vocal Band, written by L. Kirk Talley, 1992.
30. "It Is Well with My Soul," Horatio Spafford, 1873.

CHAPTER 13: GOD IS MERCIFUL

31. On the cross Jesus said, "It is finished" (John 19:30). I have read and understand this to mean

He finished paying for my sin and yours—paid in full.

Chapter 14: God Is Just

32. "Jesus Paid It All," Elvina M. Hall, 1865.

Chapter 15: God Is Gracious

33. "Amazing Grace," John Newton, 1779; *Logos Hymnal*, 1st ed. (Oak Harbor, WA: Logos Research Systems, 1995).
34. There are many efforts to define grace—about as successfully as we can describe and define God Himself. This definition, source unknown, is about as good as any.
35. The Amplified Bible is just what it says—it is an amplification or expansion upon the original language. As we have many words that have multiple meanings, the Amplified simply gives you the full feeling and meaning of the word as used in the original text.
36. Vocal artist Wintley Phipps supposes, with good reason, the melody for "Amazing Grace" came from the very people John Newton once abused before encountering the grace of God.
37. Proverbs 27:6 says, "Faithful are the wounds of a friend; profuse are the kisses of an enemy."

Chapter 16: God Is Sovereign

38. A. W. Tozer, *The Attributes of God: Deeper into the Father's Heart,* vol. 2 (Camp Hill, PA: WingSpread, 2007), 145-146.

CHAPTER 18: GOD IS HOLY

39. Arthur W. Pink, *The Attributes of God* (Grand Rapids, MI: Baker, 1975), 45.

CHAPTER 19: GOD IS FAIR

40. "Fairest Lord Jesus," Joseph A. Seiss, 1873, *Logos Hymnal,* 1st ed. (Oak Harbor, WA: Logos Research Systems, 1995).

CHAPTER 20: GOD IS RIGHTEOUS

41. "My Hope Is Built on Nothing Less," Edward Mote, 1834.

CHAPTER 21: WHO YOU ARE IN CHRIST

42. "Jesus Paid It All," Elvina M. Hall, 1865.

CHAPTER 22: HOW THEN SHALL WE LIVE?

43. "Jesus Paid It All," Elvina M. Hall, 1865.
44. Francis Schaeffer, *How Should We Then Live?* 1976.
45. Such a step or move may be God's plan, but for most of us God's call is a call for us to be who He put us here to be, right where we are.

Chapter 23: Living by the Spirit

46. In complete honesty, thinking of God's sovereignty and Romans 8:28 which says, "all things work together for good," I believe I had to go through those experiences for purposes that I may not ever know. I firmly believe part of the purpose was to begin the process of humbling me—a process that is definitely under way but with a great deal of work left for Him to do in me.

Postscript

47. In the interest of continued candor, I give running a bad name; it passed for what I call running.

Made in the USA
Lexington, KY
09 November 2019

56797380R00139